THE CHANGING FACE OF
Grimsbury

Brian Little

Robert Boyd PUBLICATIONS

Published by
Robert Boyd Publications
260 Colwell Drive
Witney, Oxfordshire OX8 7LW

First published 1999

Copyright © Brian Little and
Robert Boyd Publications

ISBN: 1 899536 34 5

All rights reserved. No part of this book may be produced, stored in a retrieval system, or transmitted, in any form or by any means, electronic, mechanical, photocopying, recording or otherwise, without the prior approval of the publisher.

OTHER TITLES IN THE *CHANGING FACES* SERIES

Banbury: Book One
Bicester: Book One
Bladon with Church Hanborough and Long Hanborough
Botley and North Hinksey
Cowley
Cowley: Book Two
Cowley Works: Book One
Cumnor and Appleton with Farmoor and Eaton
St Clements and East Oxford: Book One
St Clements and East Oxford: Book Two
Eynsham: Book One
Eynsham: Book Two
Headington: Book One
Headington: Book Two
Jericho: Book One
Littlemore and Sandford
Marston: Book One
Marston: Book Two
North Oxford: Book One
North Oxford: Book Two
South Oxford: Book One
South Oxford: Book Two
Summertown and Cutteslowe

St Ebbes and St Thomas: Book One
St Ebbes and St Thomas: Book Two
West Oxford
Witney: Book One
Wolvercote with Wytham and Godstow
Woodstock: Book One
Woodstock: Book Two
Yarnton with Cassington and Begbroke

FORTHCOMING

Abingdon
The Bartons
Bicester: Book Two
Botley and North Hinksey: Book Two
Chipping Norton
Cowley: Book Three
Cowley Works: Book Two
Easington
Faringdon and District
Iffley
Jericho: Book Two
Kennington
Littlemore and Blackbird Leys
South Oxford: Book Two
Thame
Witney: Book Two

Printed and bound in Great Britain at The Alden Press, Oxford

Contents

Acknowledgements	4
Preface	4
Introduction	6
Section 1 The Origins and Growth of Old Grimsbury	7
Section 2 Recreation and Sport	17
Section 3 Strouds, Webbs and Lesters	32
Section 4 The Livestock Market	40
Section 5 Places of Work	48
Section 6 Religion and Education	72
Postscript	96

Cover illustrations

Front: A street party at the Blacklocks to celebrate the coronation of 1953.

Back: Midland Mart's livestock market from the air.

Acknowledgements

I would like to thank the following for their help at different stages in the production of the book. Christine Kelly, Curator's Assistant at Banbury Museum; Martin Allitt, Senior Library Assistant in charge of the Banburyshire Study Centre at Banbury Library and Paul Napier and staff at the Banbury Guardian newspaper. I am also indebted to Jeremy Gibson, Banbury Historical Society for permission to reproduce material from *Cake and Cockhorse;* Ken Gibbard for the loan of the Midland Marts Prospectus; McLean Homes (South Midlands) for kind permission to photograph their housing development; Martin Blinkhorn of Blinkhorn's Photography for originals of market photographs; Barry Davis for help in identifying photographs and, in particular, my sincere thanks must go to Margaret, my wife, for kindly word processing the manuscript and offering a sounding board at all times.

I am grateful to the following for their memories of Grimsbury and for kind permission to reproduce photographs and illustrative material:

Denis Adkins	Laurie Dancer	Colin Huckins	Stanley Richardson
Cyril Aston	Violet Elliot	John Humphris	Vince and Elizabeth Spittle
David Andrew at the Bell	Doreen Essex	G Insall	John and Betty Stroud
Ernie and Agnes Barnes	Stanley and Ivy Fuller	Wendy Jordan	Aubrey Sumner
Ron Battley	Tommy Gascoigne	Norman Kearse	Ernest Thrush
Sarfraz Bhatti	Michael Gee (deceased)	Prem Khallia	Arthur Tooth
Mike Beal	Kenneth Gillett	Brenda Lukasinska	Mark Trinder
Enid Beere	Ron Grace	Raymond and Kathleen Malcolm	Mary Upton
Marjorie Bloomfield	Geoff Hawkins		Peggy Watts
Roger Bradshaw	George and Sheila Haynes	Ann Moss	Fred Welch
Isabel Brown	Muriel Herbert	Rosemary Popplewell	
Stanley and Jessie Brown	Rosemarie Higham	Mary Powell	
Pat Colgrave	Susan Hind	Doreen Prentice	

Preface

This second book is about Banbury's neighbour to the east of the Oxford Canal, River Cherwell and the railway line. It seeks to identify the people and the processes responsible for the changing character of Grimsbury.

At the time of the Boundary Commissioners' Report of 1831, the area consisted of two distinct, small and separated parts. There was Old Grimsbury which stretched in a straggling line from a wharf on the Canal to the Daventry Road and there was Waterloo, a hamlet of hovels immediately east of the bridge which connected Banbury with Grimsbury. Between the two were fields, very large in the case of the Great Meadow. Grimsbury was in Northamptonshire for much of the century and was linked with Nethercote in the Parish of Warkworth for Poor Law purposes.

Between 1831 and 1900 Grimsbury grew in response to industrial, railway and trade developments. New Grimsbury filled the fields north of the Banbury to Lutterworth Turnpike Road (Middleton Road) and expansion of streets and housing extended the area to the south of it.

Interviews with people who have spent all or part of their lives in Grimsbury take the story on into the present century. Recollections and illustrations combine to highlight the uniqueness of the area and help to account for a pride and passion that cannot fail to generate interest in the area "over the bridge".

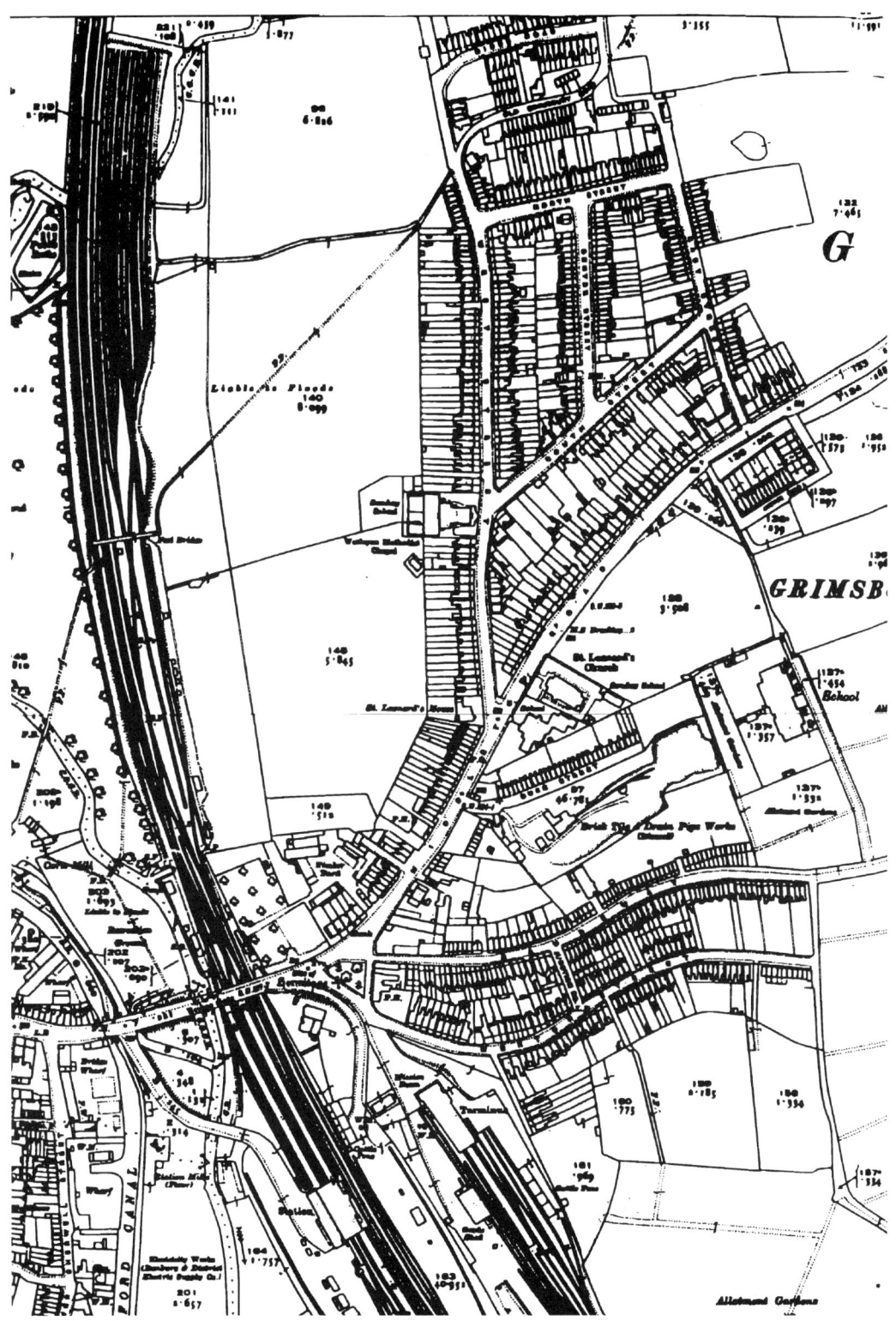

Extract from 1922 revision of 1882 O.S. map.

Introduction

A new road sign just beyond the bridge over the Oxford Canal, River Cherwell and railway exhorts the motorist to drive slowly before entering Grimsbury. Approximately this marks the beginning of the spine of the area which is the Middleton Road, on or about the orientation of the ancient Banbury Lane. In the present century it has been widely regarded as the local high street with an appropriate variety of shops and services not matched elsewhere.

Many traditional elements in Grimsbury date especially from the nineteenth century when plots of land were secured particularly from the Banbury Freehold Land Society. Builders were then engaged to develop the terraces of West, East, North, South and Centre Streets.

The working background of people in Grimsbury came to be dominated by the industries of the Cherwell area such as Samuelson's Britannia Works and by the Great Western amd London and North Western Railway Companies. Many regulars at the Elephant and Castle, the Bell, the Cricketers and the Prince of Wales were footplate men. From 1932, job backgrounds also included the operations of the Northern Aluminium Company in Banbury's Southam Road. Commencing in 1925, Midland Marts Ltd. began the process of establishing a livestock market on the edge of Grimsbury close to the railway lines. Subsequent movements of animals meant that there was a significant effect on the lives of many people in Grimsbury especially those whose homes were in Merton Street and the Causeway,

My book is not intended to be an exhaustive study of Grimsbury. It highlights some of the people and personalities who have contributed to a distinctive environment. It also takes account of the changing social mix which includes many people of different cultures and backgrounds. Asian names above small shops, the presence of a mosque in Merton Street and the multi-cultural character of Bancec (Banbury Continuing Education Council) off East Street all reflect the Changing Face of Grimsbury.

SECTION ONE

The Origins and Early Growth of Old Grimsbury

Despite the efforts of archaeologists, the location of Saxon Grimsbury is not known. One possibility is that the hamlet was in the area called "Old Grimsbury". It is here that pre-nineteenth century settlement gathered around a manor house. The original sixteenth century manor had been the home of the Cope family but it was taken down in 1836 when a new property was established for Edward Lamely Fisher. He was a farmer son of Joseph Fisher and Anne Lamely of London.

The Manor house showing evidence of former better times.

The Manor House in 1999.

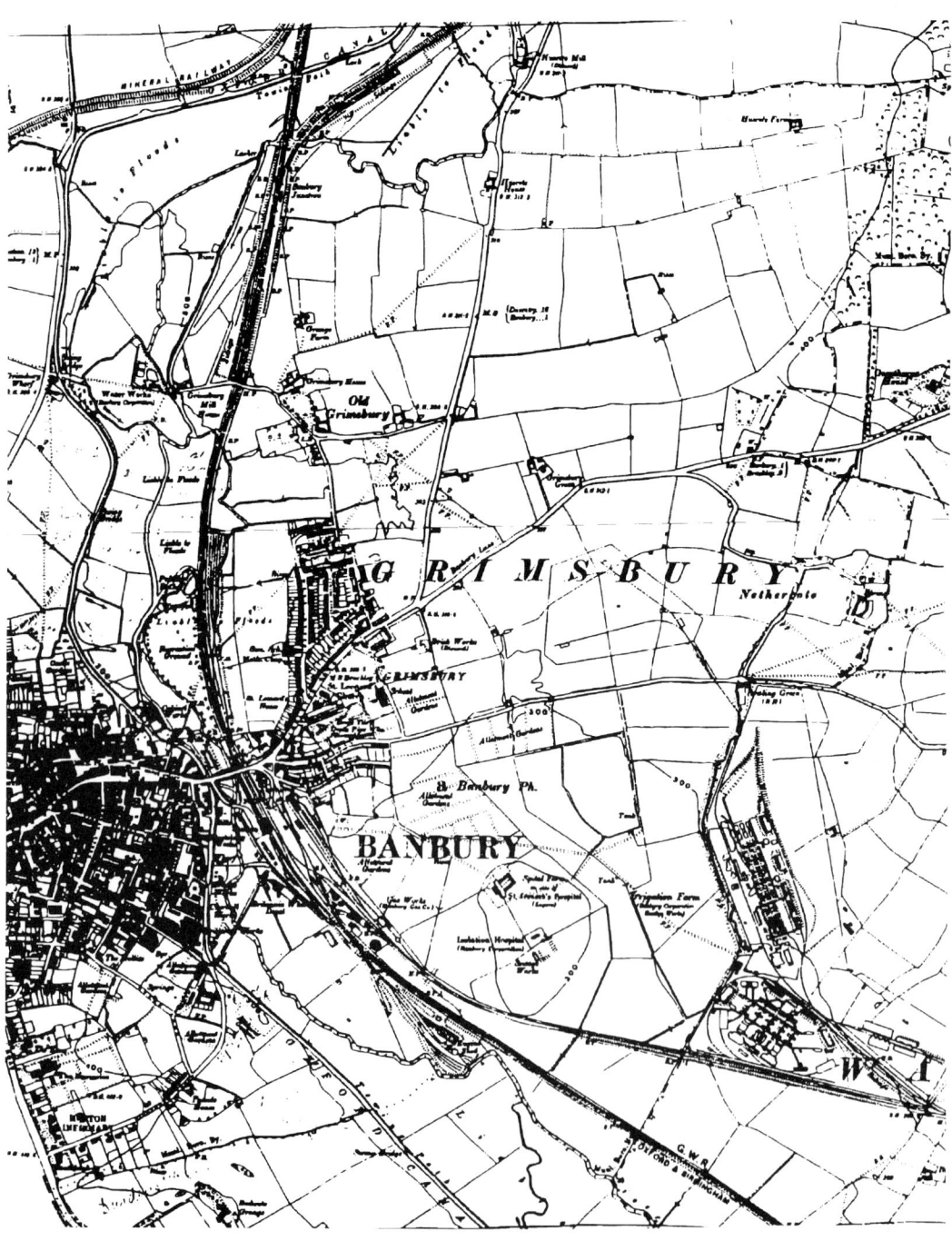

The Ordnance Survey map of 1882 shows that the house had shared property boundaries with Wildmere Farm and Manor Farm. Between 1882 and 1922 (date of O.S. map revision) there appears to have been little structural change.

THE ORIGINS AND EARLY GROWTH OF OLD GRIMSBURY

Grimsbury Manor meant a lot to Thomas Henry Gillett Pickston who was born at Altrincham in 1909 but who spent much of his life in Gibbs Road and West Street.

In the early 1920s, Thomas found Grimsbury Manor in fine condition with attractive grounds. Fountains played and peacocks strutted.

A highlight of the year at the Manor was a garden fete for St. Mary's Church organised by a Mrs. Fortesque and featuring appropriate words from Canon Jones.

In those days the Manor sported a coachman and head gardener who lived in one of the cottages opposite. Behind these was a field called Thornton's Orchard. This was where Mr. Thornton, the North Street baker, kept his horse and looked after the ponies from the big house.

Old Mill House.

Equally memorable to Mr. Pickston was Old Mill House occupied by a man called Field. Its gardens were tended by a Mr. Carter from East Street.

The eastern end of Old Grimsbury included Wildmere and Manor Farms. In September 1918, the former featured in a sale by auction of a Freehold Estate at Grimsbury Green.

GRIMSBURY GREEN,

Immediately adjacent to the important Market Town of Banbury, on the G.W.R., G.C.R., B. & C.R. and L. & N.W.R.

PARTICULARS WITH PLAN

OF AN ATTRACTIVE

Freehold, Tithe-free

ESTATE,

COMPRISING ABOUT

135 ACRES

OF EXCELLENT

Pasture and Arable Land with superior Family Residence

AND FARM BUILDINGS,

ALSO

FIELD BUILDINGS AND DETACHED COTTAGE,

To be Sold by Auction, by

MILLER AND ABBOTTS

AT THE "RED LION" HOTEL, BANBURY,

On Thursday, September 12th, 1918,

At FOUR for FIVE o'clock in the afternoon by direction of Capt. R. F. K. Gooch, M.C., and subject to annexed Conditions of Sale.

As the map shows, this included fields beyond the Daventry Road.

At the time of the sale, the farm had a tenant paying £270 a year. He was Mr. A. E. Cooke. His premises embraced a wide range of farm related buildings including a hog tub house and a granary. On the Grimsbury Green Road side there was a walled-in flower and kitchen garden and, just outside the gate, a district letter box.

In their booklet of particulars, Miller and Abbotts, who were Banbury High Street auctioneers, demonstrated an open mind about this part of Old Grimsbury. They observe that the town water is laid on and that the pasture land is very suitable for feeding and dairying purposes.

Statement of Sale.

The farm is now in the occupation of Mr. A. E. Cooke, on a yearly Michaelmas Tenancy at a rental of £270 per annum.

The Pasture Land is well watered, and very suitable for Feeding or Dairying Purposes.

The Estate lies in a ring fence, with a gentle slope to the South-west, and being within fifteen minutes walk of the Railway Stations is eminently adapted for development into a superior RESIDENTIAL ESTATE.

The Property may be viewed on application to the Tenant, and Plans and Particulars had of H. S. Knight-Gregson, Esq., Solicitor, 49, St. James' Street, London, S.W.1. (Telephone 3989 Regent), or of the Auctioneers, 30, High Street, Banbury (Telephone 35).

PARTICULARS.

ALL THAT EXCELLENT

FREEHOLD FARM

Having a frontage of over 600 yards to the Banbury and Daventry Main Road, divided into the following convenient enclosures :—

No. on Ordnance.	Description.	State.	Acreage. A. R. P.
47	Seed Ground	Pasture	20 3 1
48	Lower Ploughed Ground	Arable	15 1 17
49	Wildmere, with Cow Hovel and Yard	Pasture	4 0 10
50	Feeding Ground	Ditto	17 3 0
51	Little Breach	Ditto	5 2 20
7	Greensward Fullpit	Arable	9 1 29
8	Further Fullpit	Pasture	11 0 2
52	Ploughed Breach	Ditto	8 2 33
53	Great Breach	Ditto	12 3 28
62	Dairy Ground	Ditto	26 0 35
69	Farm Buildings, Yard &c.		0 2 29
Part 69	Cottage and Garden		
70	Paddock or Close		1 0 35
74	Dwelling House, Farm Buildings, and Gardens		1 0 26
		Acres	134 3 18

ABUTTING ON THE ROAD IS A

BRICK AND SLATED COTTAGE,

Containing Entrance Lobby, Living Room, Scullery, and Two Bedrooms, Coal and Wood House, &c., with a Large Kitchen Garden adjoining, and the CATTLE YARD near is enclosed by a high Brick Wall and 11-bay Brick and Stone Built and Slated SHELTER SHED. In Field No. 49 there is also a good CATTLE SHED, and in No. 51 a corrugated CATTLE SHED.

However there is also anticipation of future diversification into housing.

"The Estate . . . . . being within fifteen minutes walk of the Railway Stations is eminently adapted for development into a superior RESIDENTIAL ESTATE".

Manor Farm House, at the junction of Manor Road and what is now the Old Daventry Road, was built in the seventeenth century using local Hornton stone and featuring mullion windows, beams and an inglenook fireplace.

Left: Manor Farm House in snapshot view along Manor Road. Right: Manor Farm House today.

THE ORIGINS AND EARLY GROWTH OF OLD GRIMSBURY

Inglenook fireplace at Manor Farm House.

Old Daventry Road in Edwardian days.

12 CHANGING FACES OF GRIMSBURY

Apart from Old Grimsbury, the only other residential settlement of the early nineteenth century was Waterloo. This maze of hovels and dark alleyways was immediately east of the bridge which carried the road from Banbury. In 1830 there were 130 people in Waterloo. Today the name is retained for the access road to a new housing development.

Waterloo Drive During the Easter 1998 flooding.

Late nineteenth century sales of land and property provide valuable windows on the growth of Grimsbury south of the land owned by Lamely Fisher of Grimsbury Manor and north of the streets fashioned out of the territory belonging to the Freehold Land Society.

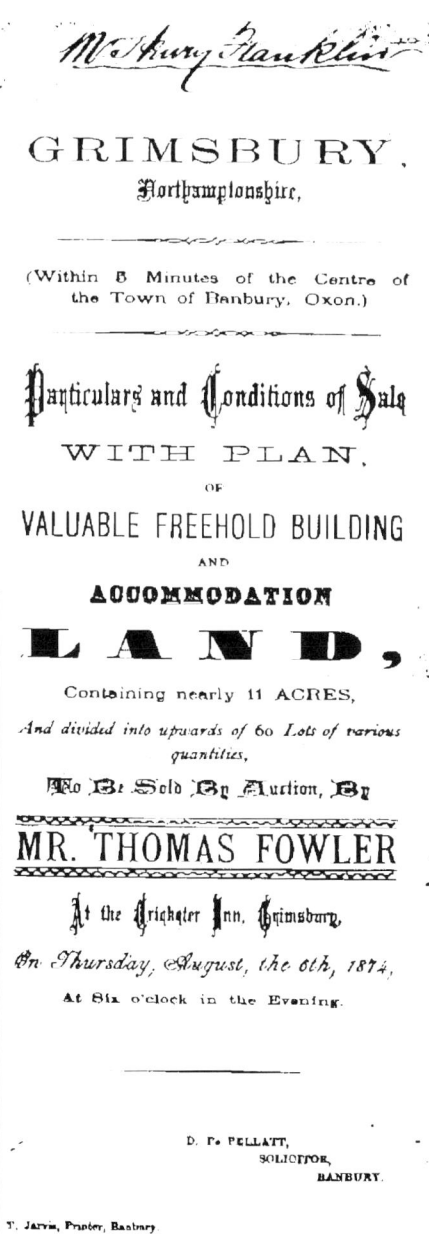

Particulars & Conditions of Sale
OF FREEHOLD
MESSUAGES, COTTAGES,
AND
BUILDING LAND,
Situate at Grimsbury in the County of Northampton, and in Calthorpe Lane in Banbury, in the County of Oxford,

Which will be Sold by Auction, by

Messrs. T. & S. ORCHARD,

At the Prince of Wales Inn, in Grimsbury aforesaid,

FRIDAY, 23RD DAY OF JULY, 1886,

At Five o'clock in the Afternoon.

Particulars and Conditions of Sale may be had of the Auctioneers, Bridge Bank, Banbury, and at the Offices of Mr. George Bliss, Solicitor, Horse Fair, in Banbury, where a Plan of the Property comprised in Lots 1 to 10 inclusive may be seen.

Particulars.

Lot 1.— All that substantially-built Dwelling House,

Containing six good Rooms (exclusive of the Bakehouse and large Storeroom over and Dairy), together with the Garden and Washhouse in the front, and a good Stable or Cowhouse and Shed near thereto, situate at the Northern end of East Street, in Grimsbury aforesaid, in the occupation of Mr. W. Gotzy. Also the SUBSTANTIALLY ERECTED COTTAGE adjoining to the said Dwelling House, with the Washhouse and strip of Garden Ground in front, in the occupation of Hours, and containing altogether 442 square yards.

There is a Well of Water in the Garden and close to the Houses, and the Water is also laid on.

The principal part of these Premises is well adapted for the businesses of a Baker and Dairyman, or either of them, and the whole are now let at the moderate rent of £25 10s 0d a year.

Lot 2.—
All that substantially-built and very convenient Cottage,

(With double front) with Yard, Court Yard, and appurtenances, situate at the Northern end of East Street in Grimsbury aforesaid, containing 91 square yards, and in the occupation of Mrs. Boswell, at the rent of £7 16s 0d a year.

In 1874, Henry Franklin who was a North Street Tailor, bought Lot 15 at an auction held at the Cricketers Inn in the Middleton Road on Thursday, 6th August. Franklin paid £11 for a rectangular strip of land between New Street (afterwards Fish Street and then Gibbs Road) and the Old Grimsbury Road. In the particulars accompanying the sale, Lot 15 was described as building land.

Twelve years later, further expansion at Grimsbury was heralded by another auction, this time at the Prince of Wales Inn, Centre Street.

14 CHANGING FACES OF GRIMSBURY

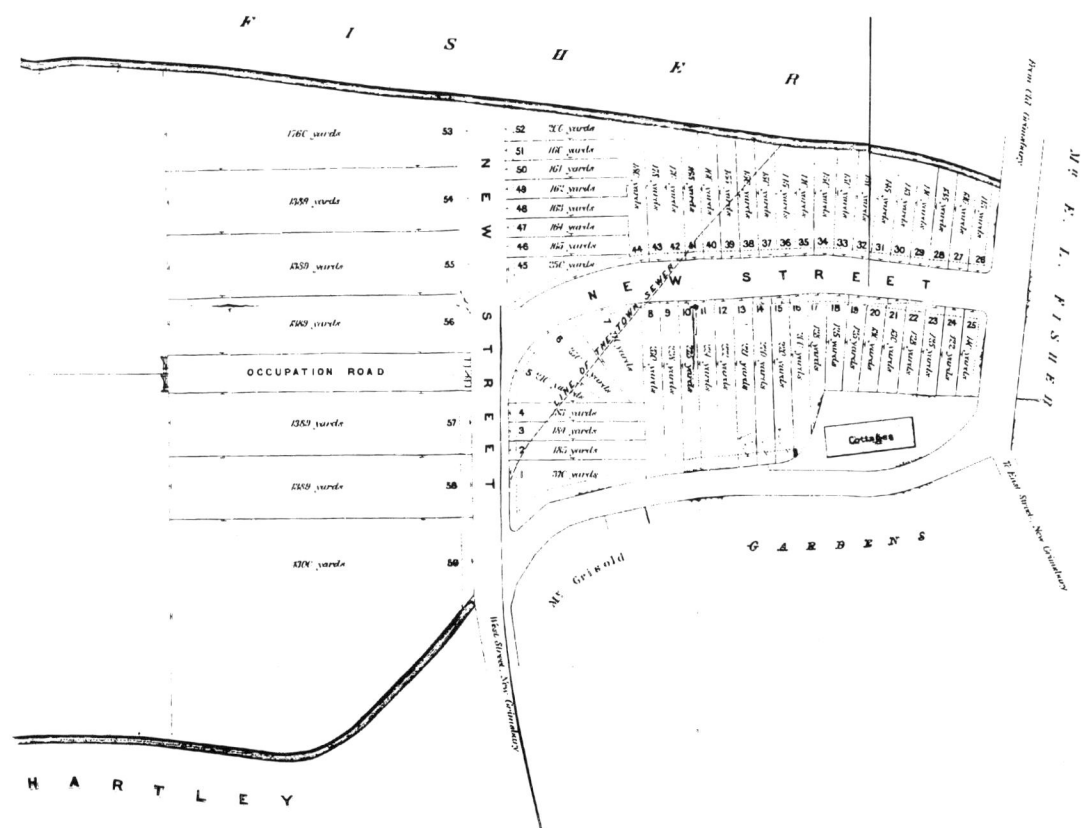

T and S. Orchard of Bridge Bank offered eleven lots, most at the northern end of East Street and near to access roads to Old Grimsbury. In an explanatory footnote, they describe the sale as, "a favourable opportunity to builders and others, and to small capitalists seeking investments for their money". This was land next to "Grisold's malthouse" where there were, six stone and thatch cottages fronting the road to Old Grimsbury, a cottage in East Street occupied by Mrs. Boswell at a rent of £7-16s-0d and nearby a substantial house comprising six rooms, a bakehouse, dairy and store, wash house and stables, all in the occupation of Mr. W. Golby.

Some of the properties in this sale had access to a spring or well and Golby's dwelling was linked to the town water supply.

In 1880, Lot 13 of the 1874 auction, was the subject of an agreement for the sale of the land for building purposes. Robert Gibbs (a Banbury fishmonger) conveyed to William Neal (boatman) in the sum of £25. It appears that this plot was part of a larger area of land earlier called the Great Meadow (over 10 acres) which had been purchased from Henry Shawe by Gibbs.

On the map accompanying the 1874 auction particulars, New Street is shown leading into West Street which was part of an emerging suburb as opposed to Old Grimsbury. From the Middleton Road northwards, development stemmed from the release of land plots for housing by the Freehold Land Society. Two examples of 1860 illustrate this trend.

The Banbury banker Timothy Rhodes Cobb sold plot 69 on South Street to Philip Chester who was a machine maker. The cost was just over £45. Clauses in the indenture point the way to subsequent house building and specifically forbid quarrying of clay and subsequent manufacture of bricks and tiles, an activity localised in the area between Duke Street and the Causeway.

Cobb also disposed of lots 109 and 111 on the Middleton Road. This time the purchaser was Joseph Scarcebrook, a Neithrop ropemaker. As in the previous example, comparable restrictive clauses appear in the wording of the indenture. An interesting feature of the accompanying plan is the recording of a tollgate, the second known to have existed in Grimsbury (the other was in the Daventry Road)

This part of the Middleton Road (between the junction with West Street and East Street was a high class section known as South Parade. A prominent resident during and after the First World War at 68 Middleton Road was Dr. Hubert De Burgh Dwyer who practised between 1915 and 1934. His work as a physician, surgeon, medical officer and Banbury District Public Vaccinator took him out and about a lot but he did not drive.

Accordingly Dwyer cast around for a chauffeur. In 1916 he appointed Richard Jarvis who had come from the St. Neots area and was lodging temporarily in Centre Street.

Dr. Dwyer and his wife, Lydia at the front door of their house in Middleton Road.

16 CHANGING FACES OF GRIMSBURY

A letter of Commendation sent to Dr. Dwyer from Frederick Bath of Roxton Park, St. Neots.

Richard was married at Sibford in 1917 and then nine years later rented an off-licence in North Street (see Recreation and Sport).

South of the Middleton Road, a working class area of properties appeared flanking the Causeway and Merton Street. This was the work of various speculators from 1850 onwards. Such builders may well have been encouraged by the mid-century arrival of railway companies. One terminus was located close to the Banbury end of Merton Street.

Richard Jarvis in his role as chauffeur, parked in Middleton Road.

SECTION TWO

Recreation and Sport

Until the recent growth of a ring of industry and new housing, the people of Grimsbury had easy contact with the countryside. "It was like a village compared with Banbury. There were fields at the end of most of the streets." This meant that children could get involved with farming occasions such as harvesting and also go searching for frogs and newts in water features that have since disappeared. Especially remembered are a little stream that flowed along the side of West Street park and a pond with tadpoles off the Overthorpe Road. Another much visited pond was in the centre of a pit left by Lampreys after their brick and tiles operation ceased on the Duke Street site. Much fun was to be had sliding down the sides of the pit on sheets of corrugated iron. It was here also that touchwood fires were made by moulding the blue clay and setting light to kindling.

The ease of walking into accessible open countryside has been recalled by Mark Trinder who was born in the Causeway and whose memories are of the 1920s. Frequently he and his family used the Middleton Road to get to Nethercote and then return via the Overthorpe Road.

On the Grimsbury side of the River Cherwell, bridges over the river and canal facilitated Sunday strolls. During these, a familiar sight was the old osier beds at the canal end of Waterworks Lane, the source of raw materials for the making of baskets intended for shopping, folding clothes and bakery purposes.

The River Cherwell itself was attractive especially to people from properties such as Mr. Field's Old Mill House. They went punting in boats maintained by Tooleys whose boatyard was at Banbury.

Punting on the Cherwell.

When the weather was very cold and the canal frozen, a great attraction for Grimsbury people in particular was to watch the many skaters who started at Field's Mill House and went as far as Banbury Lock.

Informal childhood games were often street affairs. This Beale's photograph of North Street includes two young people with possibly a home-made truck on wheels.

In the twenties and thirties with so little traffic (apart from carts), marbles, whip and top and games with hoops were popular. Some railwaymen had a metal version of marbles known as "steelies". Where balls were involved the high sides of Junction Road, which linked Merton Street and the Causeway, were well used.

Close to the gasholder which bordered the the Great Western Railway, there was a hay field suitable for informal games of football and cricket. Aubrey Sumner (born in Merton Street) was a member of a team styled the Merton Street Rangers. Their great rivals came from Edward Street and the Causeway. The former were regarded as the main opponents and no side from north of the Middleton Road appears to have had involvement.

Nearness of the field to the Market can be gauged by this view of the gasholder from across a line of empty pens.

RECREATION AND SPORT

A different informal play area was the Livestock Market. This was especially the case when snow or a big freeze meant that the children were off school for many weeks because the caretaker could not get the toilets operational. Sales rings were ideal sites for snowball fights and also games of hide and seek.

A sales ring at Banbury Livestock Market — ideal for children to play in when not in use. However these activities were not always welcomed. That well known market foreman, Henry Neal, was often seen pursuing children. Play time was not confined to daylight hours. For many it continued after dark and made use of the areas illuminated by gas lamps.

The Moors, off West Street, has a long history so far as recreation and sport are concerned. Records of Horse Racing in the Banbury Area begin in the 1720s. It is likely that the venue was Grimsbury Moors on the Cherwell flood plain as was the case early in the nineteenth century when a race course appears in the reproduction of an early Ordnance Survey map (*Courtesy E. Brown-Grant, Cake and Cockhorse Vol. 10 No.8*).

The last race was run here on 4th August 1846 when the lines of the Great Western Railway cut across the course. The Moors consisted of old enclosed ground and was sufficiently extensive to permit course expansion in 1829 when the circuit was altered to nearly two miles.

Documentary evidence shows that racing was intermittent between 1729 and 1846. Events ranged from a single day to three days and, as in 1830, had the potential to attract several thousand people, at least some of whom must have come from Grimsbury. The sources of patronage, a racing elite, were from a wider area and included the Norths of Wroxton. By contrast occupants of common lodging houses located in the nearby Waterloo part of Grimsbury put their money in the alcoholic delights of the many course side booths. This was the basic cause of serious crowd disturbances in 1843.

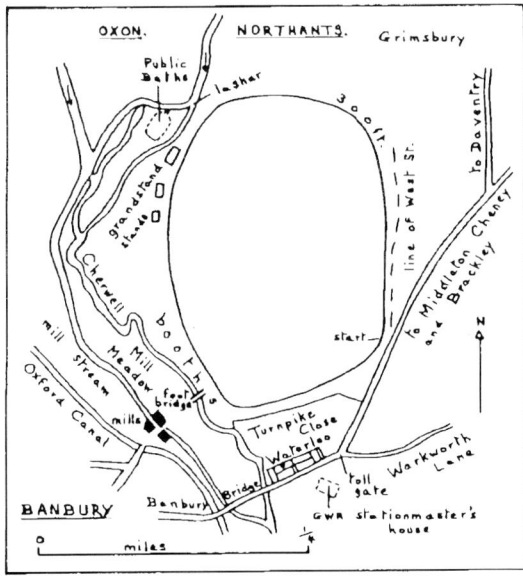

Henry Pickston recalls the popularity of this space in the 1920s. Then Stroud's field was the venue for an informal mix of cricket, football and tennis. Additionally kites were flown and these were the outcome of local enterprise. Their frames were developed at the South Street Joinery (which also acted as an undertakers) whilst appropriate string was purchased from the tent shop in the Market Place in Banbury.

The 5.79 acres known as "the Moors" was formally adopted as a recreation ground in December 1932.

In Council, the Mayor proposed and Alderman Chapman seconded the motion that the area should be purchased from the Rev'd. H. C. Hartley for £500. Trustees of the Banbury Municipal Charities contributed £200 of this.

Considering the relatively small size of Grimsbury, organised sport has been surprisingly diverse.

During the 1930s motor cycle racing took place on the site of the present Victoria Building off the Middleton Road. Well known participants were Ron Messenger, who developed his 1937 Fergusson Road Estate in Grimsbury, and Dan Surey who with his brother Bert repaired motor bikes at premises in Old Grimsbury Road.

Nearby was the Great Western Railway sports ground where both football and cricket were played.

Left: Victoria Building. Site had been used for motor cycling in the 1930s.

Right: A G.W.R. side [probably early 1930s] seen in front of their wooden pavilion on the West Street ground.

Below: British Rail team of 1975. Back row: F. Humphris, D. Barson, A. Smithson, J. Sharman, J. Hedges, G. Haynes, Mrs S. Haynes (scorer). Front row: D. Sharman, T. Wiggins, P. Hedges, L. Mawle, P. Morris, B. Coleman, W. Heighton.

Fixtures were not confined to the G.W.R. sides. For instance the printing firm of Cheney and Sons Ltd. participated in Junior League football here.

RECREATION AND SPORT

A golden oldies G.W.R. side on their football ground behind the Cricketers in Middleton Road.

School sports teams are well remembered, Grimsbury Council School soccer team of 1933-34. Back row: Norman Scroxton, ? Taylor, Cyril Buckle, ? Hunt (goalkeeper), Jim Buckle, ? Harrison, Mr. Ansell. Front row: Les Weller, Stan Fuller, Horace Gale, Lionel Hedges, Charlie Wright. Front on ground: Bob Stanton, Arthur Giles.

Grimsbury Council School Netball Team 1934. Mrs. Elliott, who was at Grimsbury Council School from 1926 to 1935, had cause to recall good netball and athletics teams. The former, as much as anything, played for the good name of the school. Members of the latter displayed their prowess on the occasion of sports days held on Harriers Field, Easington.

22 CHANGING FACES OF GRIMSBURY

Ron Grace, whose home was in Railway Terrace, Merton Street, played for St. Leonard's football team in season 1924-25

St. Leonard's soccer team 1924-25. Back row: Bert Adkins, Fred Giles, ? Impey. Centre row: Ron Grace, Len Bird, Charles Impey. Front Row: Mike Wise, Jim Sutton, Fred Turner, Phil Haynes, Charlie Tutley. Most games were away and were against village sides. Their grounds were reached by charabanc owned by Charles of Middleton Cheney.

Advertisement for yellow buses run by Charles of Middleton Cheney.

The absence of playing area facilities in Grimsbury was partly compensated by the opportunity for Grimsbury Council School to use the cricket ground of Banbury Twenty Club. Norman Scroxton, headmaster and member of the club, negotiated the arrangement,

Although the Twenty ground and facilities have always been on the fringe of Grimsbury there are many good reasons for incorporating the club into the area's history. Firstly the land used to be farmed by members of the Stroud family. Their meat was delivered by Fred Mason, a lifelong member.

Cricket teas were supplied by another club original, Ernie Lowe who spent all his life in West Street. During the fifties milk had to be fetched from the nearest farm.

The Twenty Club was formed in 1932 over a tripe supper in a back room of the Buck and Bell in Parsons Street. Those present adopted the title "Twenty Club" as that was the number in the room. The initial objective was to help train a boxer who was an early member – his name was Johny Byles.

"Old Dick" pulls the roller. Left to right: Bill Hawkins, Bill Mason and Jim Neville.

Club members' turn to pull the roller. Left to right: Fred Beasley, Wally Kearse, Eric Lowe, Maurice Varnam, Hall Holmes and George Prescott.

After a year or two changes occurred – the club base was shifted to the Wheatsheaf in George Street and cricket became the sporting focus. They acquired their Grimsbury ground in 1937.

It is perhaps especially appropriate that the first home player to score a century at Daventry Road was Bill Hawkins, founder member and tireless worker for the club.

Bill Hawkins (extreme left, front row) seen in the side of 1965.

Bill and Eric Lowe were two Twenty Club stalwarts who featured in the Banbury Nomads football team which was founded by Norman Scroxton of Grimsbury School

Nomads F.C. 1919-20. Back row: F. Shrimpton, ?, Jim Hobday, ?, C. Mold, T. Kennedy. Front row: N. Scroxton, ?, H. Walker, Eric Lowe, Bernard Blinkhorn.

Initially wanderers, their first point of stability was a ground on the Middleton Road close to the cricket. A later area side was Grimsbury United F.C. which was formed during a meeting at the Cricketers.

Much less well known is that Grimsbury had a venue for hound and whippet racing. The Banbury and District arena was established at the Banbury Spencer Sports Ground in 1933. Its location was just off the Middleton Road where a payment of 1s 0d gained admission to graded races on Tuesday, Thursday and Saturday. Every encouragement was given to local dogs.

In reviewing the past, it is clear that for some people allotment culture and not sport was allied to leisure. Prior to 1929 and the construction of Edward Street houses, a walk along the Causeway might terminate at allotment plots. As it happens these were outlasted by a site close to railside gasworks. Aubrey Sumner recalled helping to plant potatoes for which he received 6d. As he discovered, a good feature of the cattle market was the availability of manure which helped his father's crops.

The Prince of Wales public house has always been a strong focus of community interest and leisure activity.

The Prince of Wales in its Edwardian setting.

RECREATION AND SPORT

In 1855 it was the concern of one H. Claridge and, although initially only a beer house, very quickly became involved in the local Wakes which took place each July until some time in the 1860s. Mr. Claridge would roast a sheep, arrange donkey riding and provide the opportunity for music, dancing and, of course, the "imbibing of good liquors". (See Barrie Trinder's *Victorian Banbury*).

An early role for the Prince was acting as a base for the Court of the Foresters' Friendly Society. In July this Society was hosted by Joseph Harmer Kimberley in a marquee which occupied a field opposite South Street. The associated fete attracted 1,000 people whilst a procession as far as the Cross included a magical moment when the lady on a white horse threw Banbury Cakes to the waiting crowds.

These Forester festivities were happening two years after James Rusher (he compiled local directories) moved the Prince of Wales from the category of beer house to a separate list of taverns, inns and public houses. Could a spirits' licence have made the difference?

Looking through the landlords between 1855 and 1998 (the year of final closure) names that catch the eye are those of Harry Simmons and Walter James Watts.

Harry Simmons was innkeeper at the Prince, as it was always called, from 1898 to 1903. He took over the licence from Sarah Ann Pearson who had been there for two years following a move from the Town Hall Tavern in 1892.

Harry Simmonds and his family taken by Beales of Banbury in about 1903. Left to right: Margaret (daughter), Harry (father and innkeeper), George (son), Mary Ann (wife), Mary (daughter). In front: Charles (son).

At the moment of transfer (October 1898) a valuation of household furniture, fixtures, stock in trade and effects was stated at £84. 9s. 0d.

Part of the inventory.

Coincidentally an inventory was carried out covering all the rooms and spaces. The parlour had seventeen chairs; the two with arms may well have been claimed and coveted by known and accepted regulars. The effects took account of the aesthetic qualities of animal head and horns whereas four iron spittoons were highly practical.

The room layout was more formal with its seating fringing the room. Availability of beer warmers may reflect characteristic good cellarage which kept the ale cool.

The club room which had a dividing partition contained a variety of crockery, some of which had been damaged — twelve dishes and seven and a half dozen plates may have been used on some risky occasions.

The outside was interesting with its butt for catching rainwater, a pigsty (doubtless with Christmas fattening in mind), and a fenced off garden not accessible to animals.

RECREATION AND SPORTS

Wally Watts and his wife Bessy "pulling pints"; they looked after the public house from 1928 to the 1960s.

This included the very difficult war period when beer supplies might only last about two days, and the immediate post war years of shortages when a notice on the door spelt bad news for the regulars.

In Wally's days at the Prince, life revolved around a single bar, a smoke room and the jug and bottle. The bar was something of a male preserve with darts, dominoes and cribbage very much to the fore. Beer drips needed to be trapped on newspapers. Ladies mostly went into the smoke room.

Wally's great love, bowls. Pictured at the Banbury Chestnuts Club.

During the 1940s characters abounded. Prominent amongst these was George Gilkes in his brown smock – one of only a few customers who was employed at the livestock market. George was renowned for his conundrums and, when not in the Prince, could be found on his Edward Street allotment. Equally noteworthy was David of Dalbys (builders' merchants on the Banbury side of the bridge) who lived in West Street and, during the day, shovelled sand and cement.

It was David and George who organised sing-a-long groups and competed against each other except at the end of the evening when "Good Night Wally ... Good Night Bessie" floated out on Grimsbury's darkened streets.

Perhaps the prize for the greatest wit should go to Horace Williams, a carpenter who worked for Hinkins and Frewin. Few will forget his opening appeal, "Come on Wally, pint of National Health please".

A tradition at the Prince was the collection of horse race bets which were then conveyed to Horace Lester in the Middleton Road, or to George Briggs of South Street whose popular tradition was to buy everybody a drink at Christmas.

Long before Morlands took over the inn, beer was supplied by Hopecraft and Norris of Brackley and Chesham and afterwards by Phipps of Northampton.

Whatever the brew, Wally cleaned his pipes regularly and so a good pint was assured. The pub cared for its regulars but they in return contributed to the inn's reputation. Small wonder that on away days in the darts league their landlord bought the first round.

Several organisations met in the adjacent rooms and down the years these ranged from a fur and feather club to morris men.

Come 10 o'clock, Wally's boom announced no more drinks, not even for the thirstiest late arriving engine driver. If your shift was unfavourable then Northamptonshire and the Bowling Green in the Overthorpe Road beckoned.

Down the Watts years, Great Western men and many who worked for the Northern Aluminium Company were predominant customers and helped make it a lively place. Today, January 1999, the building that was the Prince, stands forlorn and boarded up, its faded sign removed. The club rooms have become houses.

The Prince after the very last orders.

RECREATION AND SPORTS

The Bell Inn in the Middleton Road was noted for the success of its 1960s Ladies' Darts Team and also for an annual race from the pub to the Three Conies at Thorpe Mandeville. The race is believed to have taken place in the late fifties and early sixties in the time of Bill Hunt as landlord. Some five people took part including Norman Coleman, Bill Upton, and Les Claridge. Bill lived in Duke Street and was a keen cyclist. Les was landlord of the Bell from 1948 and possessed a penny farthing that he rode in the race.

The victorious Ladies Darts Team: Standing: Mrs. R. Newman, Mrs. M. Saunders, Mrs. D. Knight. Sitting: Mrs. P. Pinfold, Mrs. S. Hayes (capt.), Mrs. D. Hunt, Mrs. D. Hancock.

Apart from its public houses, Grimsbury also had several off-licence premises at different times. One was run by Richard Jarvis who had come from the St. Neots area in Huntingdonshire to be a chauffeur to Dr. Dwyer. In 1925 he rented 1, North Street from the owners, Hunt Edmunds Brewery. He sold a range of beers, cider, Guiness but no spirits. Although Richard also retailed items like tea and sugar (his 1d packets were popular) he could only open in accordance with licencing hours — weekdays 10-2 and 6-10 and on Sundays 12-2 and 7-10.

Local information was available from little businesses like this. As the photograph shows, there is a poster for a cinema programme which has been placed in the window and to the right a timetable for Midland Red buses. In the 1920s it cost 1d to get from Grimsbury to Banbury Town Hall. For displaying the timetable Richard was given £1 per year by the Company.

Left: Phillip, Richard's son outside the off-licence with his Norwegian Elk Hound, Juno. The railings were taken away to melt down at the time of the Second World War.

30 CHANGING FACES OF GRIMSBURY

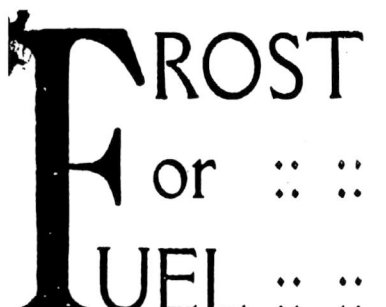

| | BEST VALUE in
Coals, Cokes,
Wood Logs,
etc. | Advert from Banbury Town and Village Directory which was kept on a hook at the 'off licence'. |

Please apply:— PERCY J. LICKORISH,

Representing—

BERNARD T. FROST

STATION APPROACH   (Merton Street)

BANBURY.

'Phone: 171.

A popular venue for leisure activities in Grimsbury was the Lido swimming pool which was reached along the Middleton Road. The pool had a fountain at one end.

The Lido showing the fountain.

RECREATION AND SPORT   31

An early event c1950's was a beauty parade; most of the participants were local girls.

The Lido shortly after closure. The notice on the fountain offers advice about articles left in the changing rooms.

SECTION THREE

Strouds, Webbs and Lesters

Today John and Betty Stroud farm land close to Hanwell Lane which connects the Coventry and Warwick roads out of Banbury. Their flight from the fringe of Grimsbury was precipitated by the coming of the M40 and marked the end of an era in which land ownership was dominated by the Stroud family whose links gave them close association with the Webbs and the Lesters.

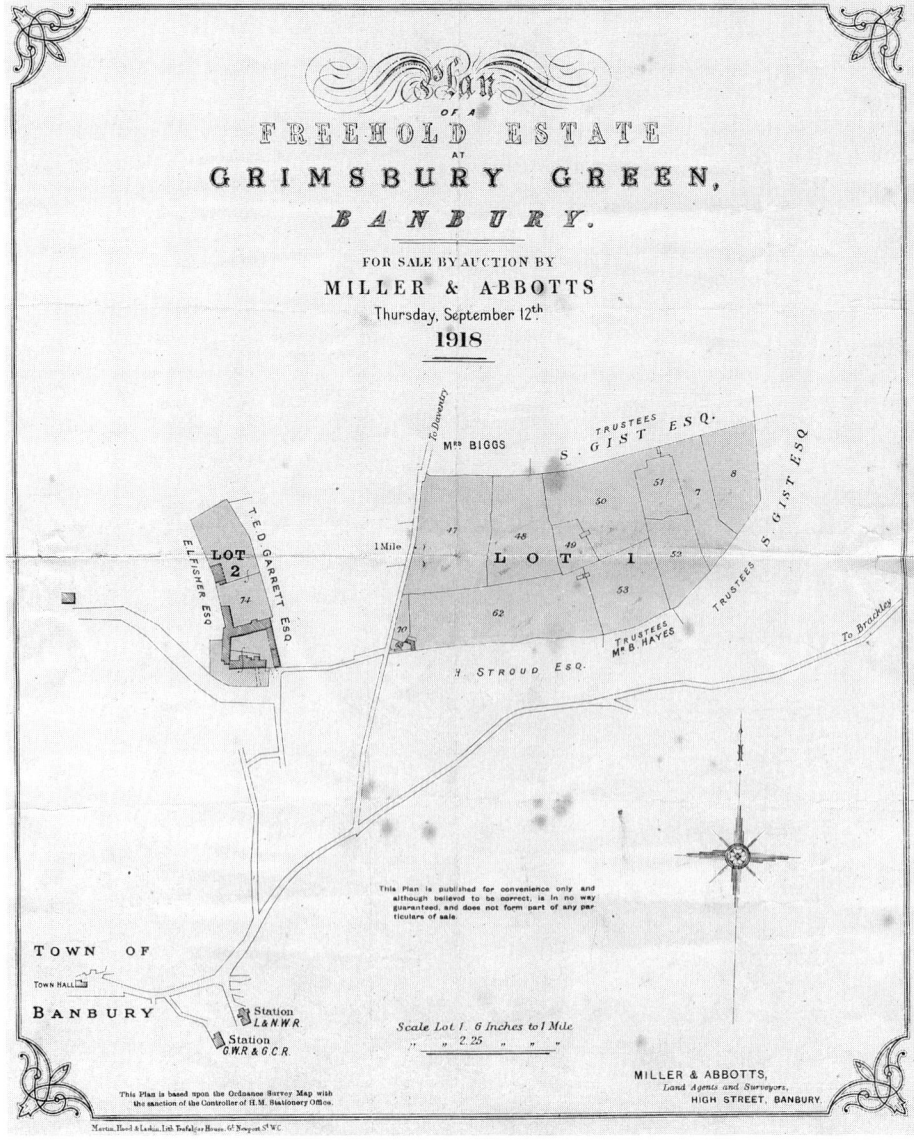

The 1918 map of the estate at Grimsbury Green includes the name of Harry Stroud across a great swath of territory in the fork between the Daventry and Brackley Roads.

This was not the only land with a Stroud name on it. Snapshots of the First World War Red Cross Hospital in West Street have a background of Stroud livestock grazing beyond the garden perimeter.

Garden of Red Cross Hospital with cattle beyond the fence.

The adjoining area of the Moors was also owned by a member of the Stroud family. Sheep grazed there were sheared by a man called Walters who had a shed for the job located near the Great Western Railway Sports Ground which took shape in the 1930s and occupied land at the rear of the West Street houses. Fred Mason, whose Bridge Street shop was featured in "Changing Faces of Banbury", worked for Bill Stroud preparing meat at the shop in the Middleton Road and later delivered the meat by horse and trap. In the photograph young Harry Stroud Junior is standing in the doorway.

Harry Stroud (junior) stood outside the family home and adjoining shop in Middleton Road.

Stroud butcher's shop customers' blotter.

In the 1940s and 1950s it was between Miss Southam (chemist) and Lampreys who sold corn and seed. Last year (1998) the need for an access road to service new houses close to the railway meant that the shop moved slightly nearer the bridge. This shop is managed by Vince Spittle and his wife.

Despite the change of location, fitments, account books, bills and blotters act as reminders of an age of personal service and area dependence on the family-run business.

Sydney Stroud, father of John had also been a farmer. He worked the land associated with Huscote Farm.

Stroud butcher's shop brass fitment.

An artist's impression of Stroud's shop.

In the picture of chain harrowing Bob Hawtin is shown with his shire horses. Bob worked for Sid and appears here with John and Bill Stroud as his youthful helpers.

Beyond the trees in the middle ground is meadow for grazing, very typical of farming in the Grimsbury area which often involved flood plain land. This was managed by Frank Colegrave. Today the land has been taken up by industry including a factory for Faccenda Chickens.

Telephone 231

The MODEL DAIRY
WEBB & SON

YOUR ATTENTION is drawn to the fact that our Bottled Milk is absolutely pure and is guarded by the "SEALED TOP"

"To think that it has come to this"!

"AS CHEAP AS ORDINARY MILK"
Butter and Eggs Fresh Daily.   Deliveries anywhere

SOUTH STREET——BANBURY

In the 1920s and 1930s Sid was also involved with a Model Dairy in Grimsbury's South Street.

He ran the business in association with Flossie who was William Webb's daughter. She began an enterprise of her own. This was the popular milk bar located in Banbury's Market Place.

Sid Stroud ouside No. 16 South Street.

The Milk Bar in Banbury Market Place.

It took some £2,000 of father's money to get the enterprise launched.

By 1940, the dairy at No. 16 South Street was under the direction of Webb and Son. Their noted specialities were "Grade A" milk from Manor Farm, double cream and Brackley sausages and pork pies. Daily from Manor Farm there were supplies of best butter and new laid eggs. The Webbs were also agents for Lyons' cakes.

During the fifties the livestock fringe of Old Grimsbury was still very much in evidence. An expanse of fields divided the space between Gibbs Road terraces and houses on Grimsbury Green.

Cows belonging to the Bull family grazing on part of this land.

Ernie Barnes of the Green has recalled how there were daily processions of bullocks and cows to behind his property. Since that time pasture has succumbed to houses, and in 1999 the last field due west of Manor Farm House has been prepared for an estate of McLean Homes.

Some of the houses which have replaced fields south of Grimsbury Green.

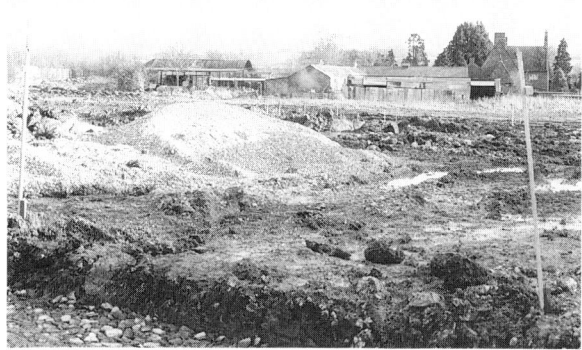

"A field of footings" for McLean Homes in Manor Road.

Important occupants this century have been the Webbs whose garden was used in 1920 for one of the grandest Wedding Day gatherings that there can ever have been in Grimsbury.

The Wedding Party in the garden of Manor Farm House.

38   CHANGING FACES OF GRIMSBURY

It is easy to appreciate why the Webbs were attracted to it and regarded the house as the manor of Grimsbury.

Thomas Pickston in his diaries describes Webb as a good farmer but noted that his land was liable to flood. Ironically once he became a member of the Borough Council (1923) his land was drained and Grimsbury's flood problems lessened.

Webb was the area's first councillor but he completed one term of office only. The issue of the cattle market's move to Grimsbury was strongly but unsuccessfully opposed by him. Before that point was reached however, Webb, as a councillor, made himself available for consultation. He met people in the Cricketers (Middleton Road) and in the Prince of Wales (Centre Street).

The Cricketers Inn (extreme right), Middleton Road, a venue for Councillor Webb's "surgeries".

One of the most notable of the Lesters in Grimsbury was Horace. Horace and his wife in his mayoral year.

Horace had two houses at different times, both called "Sunloch", named after a successful racehorse. His first property was in the part of Merton Street near the Alma Terrace. The second and more substantial was in the section of the Middleton Road known as the South Parade.

The Parade today — still impressive.

This was very much a business and professional community between the West and East Street junctions. Neighbours of Horace and Lester were bank and brewery clerks, a doctor, a surveyor, a draper and an excise officer.

Horace himself was a bookmaker. Each day he took all the main racing dailies. These were delivered by the newsagent on the Bridge and there was an expectation that the papers would be through his door by 7.45 a.m.

Amongst those who placed bets with Horace were regulars at the Prince of Wales in Centre Street. Wally Watts, the renowned landlord for some thirty years from the early 1930s, had a bag for the punters' papers and someone was relied on to run back and forth from the pub to Sunlock.

The Middleton Road house was very large and the garden stretched back to South Street. It contained apple trees and these were a target for marauding school boys, at least until P.C. "Bandy Merritt intervened. His leather gloves inflicted a painful blow to the ears which encouraged his "victims" to surrender the fruit tucked under pullovers.

At Christmas, "Sunlock" was Mecca for the Lester family. No seasonal gathering was complete without a ceremonial bearing of the turkey from Jelf's bakery in South Street to Horace's table.

H. S. LESTER & SONS LTD
Turf & Football Accountants.
Established 1908
Members of Victoria Club
N.S.L. & B.P.A.
Tel: 2233 (8 lines)

BANBURY'S LARGEST BOOKMAKERS
with branches at
BRACKLEY, BUCKINGHAM, BYFIELD, CHARLBURY, CULWORTH, TINGEWICK
All business strictly private.
BET WITH AN OLD ESTABLISHED AND RELIABLE FIRM.

"SUNLOCH", BANBURY

SECTION FOUR

The Livestock Market

The establishment of Banbury Livestock Market by Midland Marts Ltd. in a part of Grimsbury adjacent to the lines of the Great Western and London and North Western railway companies was very much a farmers' movement.

In part it was a response to the situation whereby in the Banbury of 1919, buyers and beasts had become mixed up with motor buses, cars, carriers carts and passing traffic of all descriptions.

Ten years later the prospectus of Midland Marts Limited reveals that of nine members of the Board of Directors, five were farmers, one was a big landowner at Farnborough, one a stockbroker and there were two auctioneers.

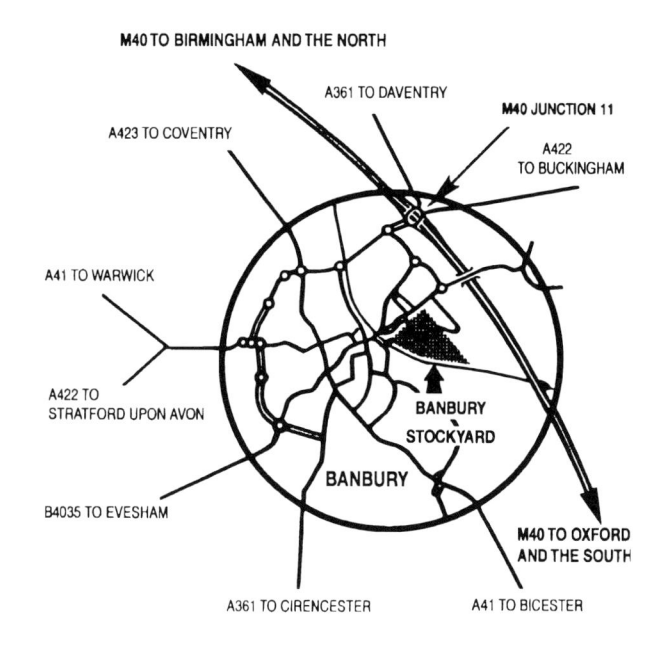

Not one of these appears to have been connected with Grimsbury though company shares were offered to people living in Merton Street.

The driving force behind the enterprise was Alexander Patrick McDougall of Prescote Manor near Banbury. This Scotsman had the vision to appreciate that the location was likely to make the market a mecca for buyers and sellers.

The decision about the Grimsbury site became a government one. On 2nd April 1925, Edward Wood, Minister of Agriculture, declared the new enterprise open. This action inspired a letter written to the Banbury Guardian which appealed for purer language in the new market than had been the norm with street gatherings.

Appropriately the very first sale opened with the donation of a heifer by Major Crossley of Wykham. The money from the sale was given to the Horton Infirmary Extension Fund. Later that day, there were prizes amounting to £58 and cattle, sheep, pigs and calves were all displayed, as the publicity said, in iron pens.

Down the years, the market has seen a transition from locally based sellers to support from across the country. In particular, and from about 1931, Banbury Stockyard became a centre for old cows and large numbers of these went to Sheffield to supply the canning business. A farming association with our area was provided by the Basingstoke Holtons. They were responsible for train-loads of cattle which came into Merton Street station.

A COPY OF THIS PROSPECTUS HAS BEEN FILED WITH THE REGISTRAR OF COMPANIES.

The Subscription List will close on or before the 30th day of September, 1929.

None of the Shares of this Issue have been underwritten.

MIDLAND MARTS LIMITED

(Incorporated under the Companies Acts 1908 to 1917).

SHARE CAPITAL £33,000

DIVIDED INTO

50,000 ORDINARY SHARES of 10/- each, and

8,000 6% PREFERENCE SHARES of £1 each

of which there have been issued

30,690 ORDINARY SHARES of 10/- each   £15,345.

Issue of 8,000 6% Preference Shares of £1 Each at Par

BARCLAYS BANK LIMITED, BANBURY, and all Branches, are authorised to receive applications on behalf of the Company for the above-mentioned Preference Shares payable as follows:—

    On Application - - 5/- per Share.
    On Allotment - - 5/- do. on October 1st.
    and the balance on October 28th, 1929.

Preferential allotment will be given to applications received from existing shareholders of the Company, provided application is received on or before 31st August, 1929.

The minimum subscription on which the Directors will proceed to allotment is 5,000 Shares.

The holders of the Preference Shares are entitled to be paid out of profits for each year a preferential dividend for such year at the rate of 6 per cent. and in the event of the Company being wound up will be entitled to have the surplus assets of the Company applied in the first place in repaying to them the amount paid up on the Preference Shares and any arrears of dividend up to the commencement of the winding up whether declared or not but will not be entitled to any further participation in such surplus assets.

Every shareholder of the Company whether Preference or Ordinary is entitled at meetings of the Company to one vote on a show of hands and on a poll to one vote for every share held by him/her.

Dividends will be payable half-yearly on 1st May and 1st November. Three months' interest will be payable on the 1st November, 1929, on the amount paid on allotment of Shares.

Payment in full may be made on allotment interest at the rate of 5% per annum being allowed in respect of the prepayment of the final instalment due, on 1st October, 1929. Interest at 10% per annum will be charged on all overdue instalments and failure to pay the balance when due on shares allotted will render previous payments liable to forfeiture.

Directors:

ALEXANDER PATRICK McDOUGALL, C.B.E., Prescote Manor, Banbury, Farmer—Chairman.
ERNEST ABBOTTS, F.A.I., Broughton Road, Banbury, Auctioneer.
MAJOR ERIC CROSSLEY, O.B.E., Wykham Park, Banbury, Farmer.
JOHN EDWARDS, 102 Turnpike Lane, Hornsey, London, Butcher and Farmer. (Vice-President National Federation of Meat Traders' Association).
GEORGE GIBBARD, Crouch Farm, Banbury, Farmer.
WILLIAM ISAAC RICHARD LIDSEY, Hardwick Farm, Banbury, Farmer.
PERCY CLARKE MILLER, F.A.I., Broughton Road, Banbury, Auctioneer.

Bankers:
BARCLAYS BANK LIMITED, Banbury.

Solicitors:
FIELD, ROSCOE & Co., 36, Lincolns Inn Fields, London, W.C.2.

Auditors.:
THOMSON ALLISON & WILSON, Chartered Accountants, 29 Great Pulteney Street, W.1.

Secretary and Registered Office:
F. BLISS, 30 High Street, Banbury.

Page of Prospectus for 1929 share issue.

Characteristic views of livestock in pens taken in the 1950s.

The Railway

Merton Street station was the nearby terminus of the London and North Western Railway (later L.M.S.)

THE LIVESTOCK MARKET   43

Left: a one coach diesel unit at the station. Right: a poster announces the switch from steam to diesel — it failed to prevent closure.

Merton Street station after closure.

Livestock from many sources were held overnight in fields beyond the built up area of Grimsbury's Causeway and Merton Street. Midland Marts used fields both close to Grimsbury (for more immediate sales) and further away near Overthorpe (for less imminent sales). Notably animals were grazed on a block of land north of Overthorpe House and including certain fields surrounding Gilbey's cottages.

Dairy Ground, Palmers Green, Thornton and Seed Field were well known to those who escorted livestock.

Cattle, sheep and pigs were driven to market through the Causeway and Merton Street and an inter-connecting lane. Drovers hurried them along with shouts, sticks and the aid of a dog. With cattle such an ever present fact of life in Merton Street and the Causeway, residents were allowed to keep their own iron railings despite wartime demands for the metal. On occasions not even these were an adequate protection.

Vera Elliot, whose family home was in the Causeway, recalled the day when a Hereford bull got stuck in their yard while her mother was busy mangling a sheet in a shed. Another incident, well-remembered by her, involved a bull and Harry Neal the market foreman. He was pursued up the Causeway and only escaped by suddenly swinging round a lamp post as the beast careered past him. Harry could run hard despite having one leg shorter than the other.

Vera Elliot of the Causeway had vivid memories of the market and its movements.

Harry Neal stands on the auctioneer's right.

Right: Tony Phipps pushes out the pigs.

On the whole people learnt to live with the market though they never liked it because of the noise and mess and always looked forward to Friday because it was the day when the council disin-fected both street and pavement.

Numerous representations were made to the council but this was to no avail – elected members saw the market as an income generating asset. Another and more romantic view of it was supplied to Sarah Gosling (a former Banbury Museum Curator) by a M. Bloomfield who said, "My most vivid memories of the market are of steaming cattle on wet days, warm farmyard smells and the sweet, sickly odour of horses".

The same person recalled a character of a drover who lived in Edward Street. He was a little man with a permanent dribble. Sporting a trilby hat to keep off rain or as a protection against the sun, he carried a hickory stick to help herd the beasts to market as he walked along in his dung-covered boots.

Drovers were not the only people involved with livestock movements. Sometimes local children helped. Aubrey Sumner remembers taking cows from the Market to the fields. This involved a journey up Rocky Road from Merton Street to the Causeway and then along the Overthorpe Road on either side of which there was grazing. It was worth the effort to get 3d a journey.

Left: Flocks of sheep in pens.

46 CHANGING FACES OF GRIMSBURY

Top: Geoff Curtis (left) a farmer from Ashingdon near Aylesbury.

Second down: Bill Harvey from Norwich who came over on Wednesdays.

Third down: William Lombard (left) of Chacombe whose family had attended since 1925, Bill Cooper (right) from Hertfordshire.

Bottom: Robert Gray (left) farmer from Hertfordshire and Charlie Reading – Drover (right), together on day of sale of effects.

During the 1930s, the market suffered many hiccups. Chief amongst these was a foot and mouth scare which interestingly turned into an opportunity to demonstrate that stock went to as many as 310 countries.

On the plus side, 1936 saw the additions of a corn exchange at the saleyard. Previously corn sales had been focused on the Red Lion and Crown, both in Banbury. A century earlier there had been two exchanges in the Market Place.

World War ll restrictions on livestock movements were a problem. Only cattle within a ten mile radius could come to the market which was not central to a main grazing area for the fat cattle that had been nine tenths of the trade.

After the war, and by the mid-fifties, personalities of the stockyard were well established.

In 1957, Ralph Tickle was age 90 and Stan Gage had had some thirty years experience of selling fat cows. Jack Hart and W.A.C. Southgate were well known auctioneers and Charlie Arbon was remembered for his use of a loudspeaker instead of a bell for summoning buyers to the start of a sale.

THE LIVESTOCK MARKET

Midland Mart records show that in 1956 some 219,000 animals were handled at the market. This compared with 9,000 in 1924. No wonder that McDougall's "Magnificent White Elephant" had inspired him to observe in the mid 50s, "By God we've made their town".

During the Second World War, the market space was used by the Home Guard. Many of its members lived in Grimsbury. These people trained but they also had a band that played on the open area flanked by the banks.

On the recreational side of the Midland Mart operation there was some involvement in cricket (office staff) and football. Prior to the 1960s, there was an annual soccer fixture with lorry drivers at New Milton in Hampshire. An interesting aspect of an all friendlies programme was that the side played in claret and blue. Quite by chance, some cheap shirts were found in a remainder bin at a sports' shop in Banbury's Palace Arcade.

The Livestock Market closed on June 4th 1998 — the end of an era for the people of Grimsbury. For a while there was the prospect of a new location at Huscote Farm but that chance has now gone with the sale of the land.

Model of the proposal to develop the Huscote Farm site.

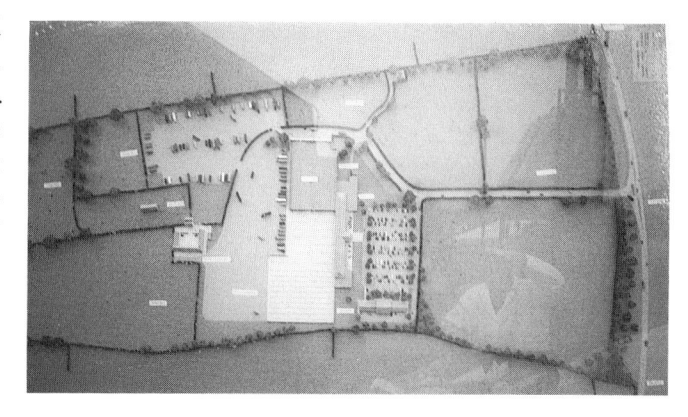

The very last animal (a Charolais) leaves the sale ring watched by auctioneer Jim Watts.

SECTION FIVE

Places of Work

The Ordnance Survey Map of 1882 shows that brick manufacture and associated activity was widespread in urban North Oxfordshire. A prime location was in Grimsbury between Duke Street and the Causeway. Here Lamprey and Sons had a large works of over 3,000 acres which was based on an outcrop of Oxford Blue Clay. It produced tiles and pottery as well as bricks.

Lamprey's brickworks with Causeway terraces in the background.

Work in progress at Lamprey's brickworks.

PLACES OF WORK 49

Lamprey's carter near the brickworks, 12,000 moulded bricks a day were turned out from two kilns.

There was a shed for the drying process and this had a heated floor. In summer bricks were dried out of doors.

Lampreys owned half of nearby Duke Street which had been a speculative development of 34 houses. The other half of the street was in the ownership of Noel Robins, a Banbury Market Place ironmonger.

Manufacturing activity ceased early in the nineteenth century and a large residual pit became home to the local children who used it as an informal adventure playground (see section on Recreation and Sport).

During the 1880s and 1890s, and according to Barrie Trinder in his "Victorian Banbury", the only other source of industrial employment was a perambulator works, not located.

A Lamprey's brick.

Munitions Factory

During the First World War and for a brief period afterwards, a significant place of employment was the National Filling Factory No. 9. It was located on the Overthorpe side of the area and had access to the London and North Western railway line which ran into Merton Street Station.

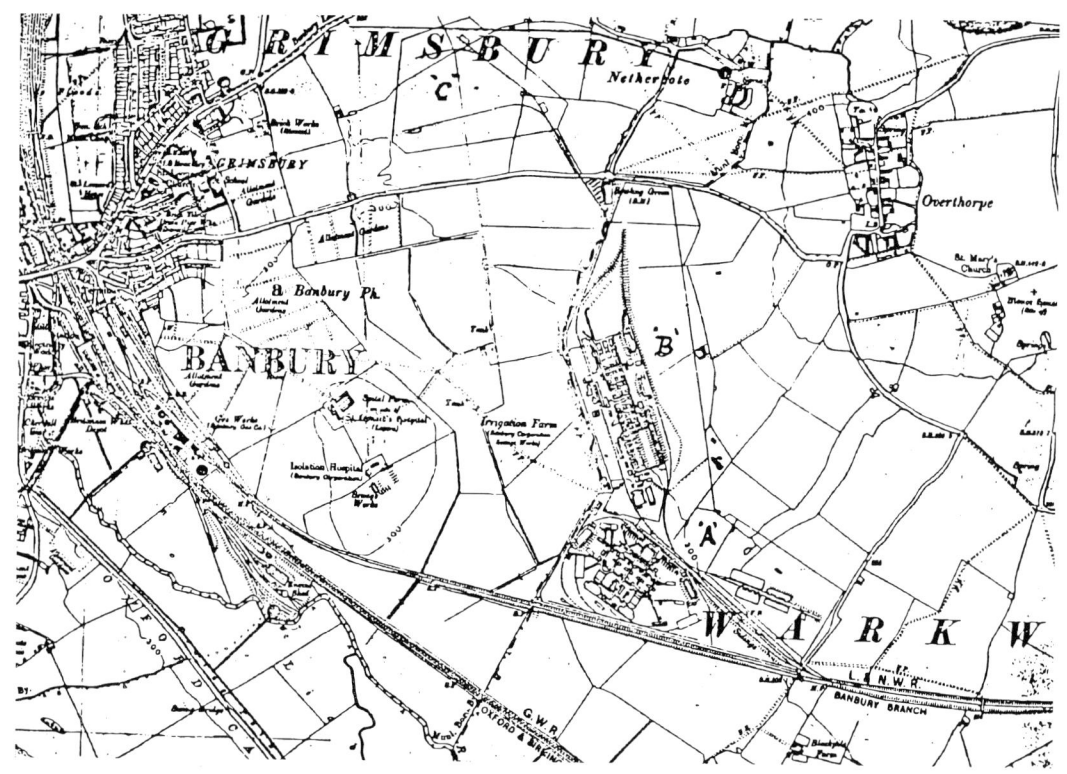

Layout of National Filling Factory.

Production of filled shells began in April 1916 and provided jobs for 933 men and 548 women at the height of wartime activity. A typical busy week ended on 3rd March 1917 with a total output of some 7,000 of the 9.2 inch shells.

Key staff of the factory were headed by a works manager who was Captain Snowball. Chief Foreman was Mr. Berridge, engineman was Mr. Bedlow, maintenance fitter Mr. Viggers and the fire officer was called Dicker.

Activity along the production line was in the form of shift work for which the average pay was £1 5s. 9d per week, whilst for nights people could earn £1 10s. 3d. There were bonuses ranging from 3s. to 16s. a week for additional production.

Trolley girls could get 6d. extra a day and 9d. more at night. If shells were a bit out of the ordinary then you were known as a special powders woman which meant 2s. extra per week and hot cocoa or milk twice per shift.

The working environment of the sheds was very clean and well lit. Operatives kept warm and dry in steam heated areas as they moved about in their fire-proof clothing. Female trolley pushers sported khaki trousers and tunics whilst powder handlers of the same sex were turned out in tunics, hats and white trousers.

Powder had to be treated with great respect as it could be an irritant. No surprise therefore that the filling factory had a surgery with soothing powders and lotions. The other problem was that they could discolour the skin. Handling of them took place in the yellow rooms and the women became known as the canaries.

Steam engine "John" — work horse of the Filling Factory.

The support railway system was likened to a Hornby layout over which saddle tank engines John and Lidban chugged their steaming way.

Factory closure came in 1924 but employment levels had dropped well before then. The National Filling Factory was not revived in 1939, instead the site was used by the army and the home guard.

Paxmans of South Street

In 1919 William Paxman came to Grimsbury from Lismore in Southern Ireland. He founded a milk business in South Street but, after a bried period of two years, he turned to butter manufacture.

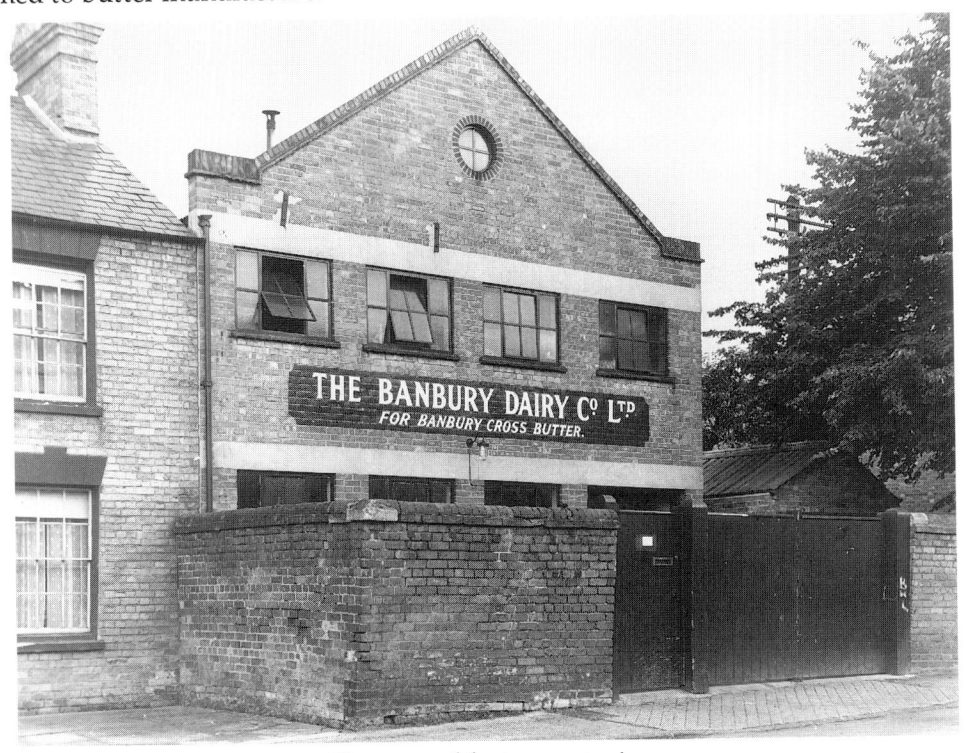

Close up of factory exterior.

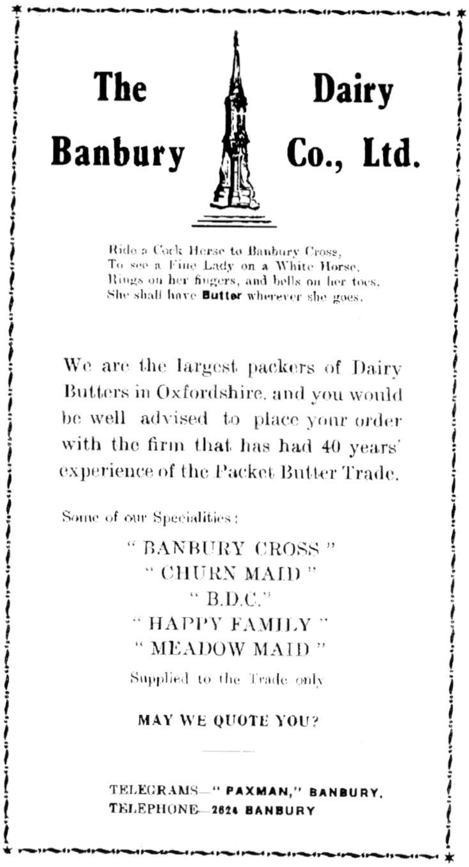

> **The Banbury Dairy Co., Ltd.**
>
> Ride a Cock Horse to Banbury Cross,
> To see a Fine Lady on a White Horse,
> Rings on her fingers, and bells on her toes.
> She shall have **Butter** wherever she goes.
>
> We are the largest packers of Dairy Butters in Oxfordshire, and you would be well advised to place your order with the firm that has had 40 years' experience of the Packet Butter Trade.
>
> Some of our Specialities:
>
> "BANBURY CROSS"
> "CHURN MAID"
> "B.D.C."
> "HAPPY FAMILY"
> "MEADOW MAID"
>
> Supplied to the Trade only
>
> **MAY WE QUOTE YOU?**
>
> TELEGRAMS—"PAXMAN," BANBURY.
> TELEPHONE—2624 BANBURY

Company Advert in Banbury Official Guide.

This was not a casual decision as he had a lot of experience in Ireland working alongside his brother.

The enterprise of William and Richard Paxman (his son) was a modest one.

At most 10 other people were involved, The blending process occupied the attention of half of these. Then there were three ladies in the offices and two representatives to maintain contacts within a market area which embraced Banbury and villages up to about twenty miles distant. The movement of products could be managed in one delivery van. As the photograph shows it had appropriate logos.

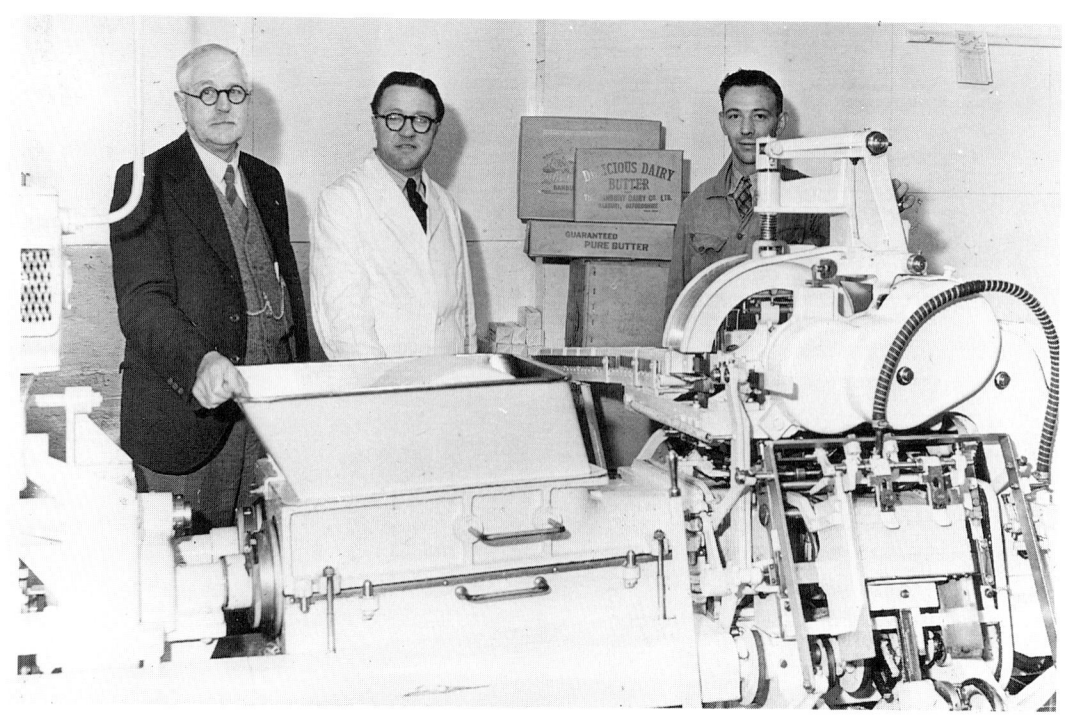

William (left) and Dick (centre) on the factory floor.

PLACES OF WORK 53

The Paxmans had a close link between home and factory. They lived at 145 Middleton Road, conveniently next door to Dr. Winn, and backing on to the business. Access for their deliveries was in South Street and Denis Adkins, who traded in fruit and vegetables, has memories of lorries coming from the railway station with supplies of foreign fat. Cherry's of Cropredy had a lorry link between Paxmans and the Cold Store close to the Waterworks in Old Grimsbury.

The Paxmans sent their packets of butter, which were destined for retailers beyond Banbury, in large boxes. These were made attractive in themselves and had clever design work as well as an appropriate variation of the local nursery rhyme:

The delivery van caught on camera near Banbury Cross. One slogan is clearly visible but on the other side of the lorry it said, "Don't pass a good butter — BUY".

Ride a Cock Horse to Banbury Cross
To see a fine lady ride on a white horse.
Rings on her fingers and bells on her toes
She shall have butter wherever she goes.

Paxman's butter business left Grimsbury for Castle Street, Banbury, in the 1950s. The attraction was larger premises. Meanwhile back in Grimsbury the former building appears much the same, that is except for users.

The building today. Sign boards indicate very different activities.

Banbury Cold Store

Banbury Cold Store in Grimsbury was built early in World War ll. It was part of a chain of 48 stores belonging to the Ministry of Food who saw the town as a relatively safe haven. Ministry officials supervised the work which was based on six cold rooms containing a variety of items such as lamb, mutton, bacon, eggs and corned beef. Apart from this main part of the store, there were six sheds with a capacity of 3,000 tons of dry goods.

The Cold store.

Assorted Sheds.

A typical cold room.

PLACES OF WORK 55

Considering the thousands of tons of food stored, it is not surprising that labour force recruitment meant looking beyond Banbury. Several key men came from London. Included amongst these was Mr. A. Hayne who became manager in 1954. Chief engineer and later manager was Mr. B. Clargo who lived in Gibbs Road.

Transit of goods.

Mr. B. Clargo inspects machinery.

The Cold Store area today.

Shops

Throughout the present century the small shop has been a place of work in most Grimsbury streets. A good example was the front room business of Arthur and Eleanor Hobbs at 45 Centre Street which dated back to the early 1900s.

Eleanor Mary Hobbs and son outside shop in Centre Street and in the garden.

From their property halfway along the east side, they sold sweets and soft drinks and were the first Hobbs family link with paraffin sales. It is believed that the shop was also an outlet for secondhand china.

PLACES OF WORK   57

Some retail activity in Grimsbury was linked to an associated distribution business. Especially notable from 1930 to about 1960/61 has been the Adkins family. They had a nursery in the Overthorpe Road.

Top: Aerial view of Adkins nursery. It comprised of four acres of land, given over partly to green-houses with hot and cold frames.

Middle and bottom: Green-houses and frames.

Vegetables regularly included some six to seven tons of tomatoes and there were flowers such as iris and gladioli. Dearing and Barnes succeeded to the nursery land and today Nicholls (builders merchants) now occupy the site.

The produce was picked into baskets and small quantities of it went to people like Eeles of West Street who traded in fruit and vegetables.

From 1936 to 1940 the family had a horse and cart for door to door deliveries in Grimsbury. Bill was the name of the horse and he had been purchased from Bill Maris who had a sweet shop in Broad Street, Banbury. The cart was constructed by Ted Knowles, a G.W.R. train driver, who did this work as a hobby in his Edward Street back garden.

The cart was replaced with a Ford van bought from Young's Garage. The choice of this particular van stemmed from a day trip to Fords at Dagenham (1938 or 1939) organised by Mr. Young.

Adkins delivery service operated on four days each week, Tuesday, Wednesday, Friday and Saturday. When Denis was in charge of the Grimsbury round, he used to finish at Thacker's General Store in Centre Street that was nearly opposite the Prince of Wales. Thacker would buy what was left of his produce, especially rabbits and boiling fowl. The former came fresh twice a week from a man called Gregory at Heythrop. Rabbits cost 1s. each; boiling fowl sold at 2s. 6d. and roosters for 3s. 6d.

Outside of the Middleton Road, the Causeway has been home to several small but significant retail businesses.

In Kenneth Gillett's time, in that street, the 1930s and early 1940s, these included Eeles (see Grimsbury bakers) and the hairdressing business of Norman Johnson.

Norman Johnson in his Samuelson days — 2nd row, third from front left.

The latter gained experience of this kind of work by acting as lather boy for Coleman and Sons at No. 46 North Bar Banbury. The young Norman stood on a box to soap the faces of the men.

His own first salon was the front room of the family home where children earned pennies by cleaning the floor every Sunday morning.

Premises separate from where he lived were later found in Duke Street. Here Norman served both sexes. He did waving for women's hair using curling tongs which had been tested on paper to see if they were too hot. Most of the customers however were men and boys. A hair cut and shave cost 4d. but children's hair was only 2d a sitting.

Centrally placed for both the Causeway and Merton Street was the butcher's shop of Franklin's. Quality meat made it popular. When the shop closed it turned into a secondhand business.

Catharall sold mainly sweets but had a slot machine that was especially popular with children. Insertion of a farthing produced a disc on which was marked the entitlement to his confectionary.

In the Causeway, a man with a limp called Wallis kept groceries but also sold fish and chips and faggots and peas.

By contrast with the Causeway and indeed all other Grimsbury streets, the Middleton Road has generally been regarded as the high street of the area. This was certainly true of the period from 1920 to 1940.

There were some notable and mainly successful traders offering a variety of goods and services. To some extent this had been true of Edwardian times.

Edwardian postcard of the Middleton Road.

Well remembered businesses from the 1920s and 1930s include the chemist's shop of Anne Southam; the corn and cattle cake firm of Lampreys; Strouds the butchers (see section on the Stroud Family); Kirkland for cycles and Webb for confectionary (later Jelfs) followed in quick succession.

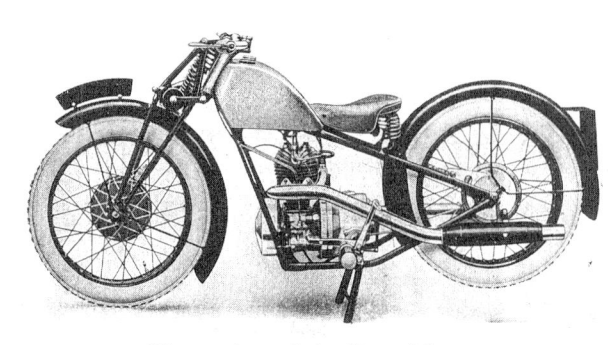

Illustration of the Berwick.

Kirkland was like Mumford in that he dealt with radio accumulators. An interesting additional piece of optimism was his acquisition of one of the only two motor cycles made by the Station Approach company of Berwick. In 1929 he secured this from the police who had in turn dispossessed two youths of it in the Warwick Road. Kirkland dismantled it and sold the various bits for parts.

PLACES OF WORK

Edith Giles kept a fruit and vegetable shop just short of the Cricketers.

One of the most successful branches of the Banbury Co-operative Industrial Society was the Grimsbury Co-op (below).

A Mrs. Cakebread was in charge of the Grimsbury Post Office but by 1940 she had been succeeded by Dorothy Barnes. Between the Co-op and the Post Office was a bakery (see section on Bakeries). Four doors from West Street was the home and confectionary business of the "Happy" Waltons. The family comprised two brothers and a sister. One of the brothers was on the short side and always appeared to be smiling. The sister worked as a cashier at the Grand Cinema in Broad Street, Banbury.

Before the turn into West Street came the residence of Mr. and Mrs. Adkins who were potato farmers at Middleton Cheney. In Grimsbury itself they did a milk round with a horse and cart.

Garages

Garages have been a feature of the east side of the Middleton Road, varying in number and location down the years. The Lido Service Station, Grimsbury Motors, City Motors, Bridge Motors have all contributed to the street scene, but undoubtedly the most outstanding in local memories was the business of George Mumford. Mumford was about five feet tall, squat and had streaky grey/silver hair. A quiet man he always had a cigarette dangling and wore an old brown smock.

VAT No. 120 1039 43				
Telephone: BANBURY 3848	INVOICE		No.	4002

THE LIDO SERVICE STATION
(Proprietors: F. H. UPTON, E. R. THOMAS)
MIDDLETON ROAD, BANBURY, OXON.

Date (Tax Point) 13.7.79

To: Mr. Dlargo

Make: VAUXHALL   Chassis No.   Colour
Reg. No.: WKX 966M   Speedo Reading: 66716   VAT Rate

To:			
M.O.T.	—	4	50
Fitting new steel brake pipes. Bleeding system		6	00
3 Steel Brake pipes.		3	38
Brake Fluid	—		55
		14	43
V.A.T. 15·1		1	40
Terms: Strictly Nett		15	83

A 1979 invoice produced by The Lido Service Station.

PLACES OF WORK 63

Until recently Bridge Street Motors occupied the large low building.

Mumfords Garage 1967, Tom Gascoigne's 1922 Fiat outside, Tommy ran the garage for 28 years.

Beginning of the end for Mumford's Garage.

George had four petrol pumps and did repairs. He was not always available to work on a car but was happy to offer the use of his tools to a known customer. If the job involved changing a wheel, George's hand strength was sufficient.

He began by selling cans of petrol from a corrugated iron hut. The cost of establishing these premises was met in part by the Strouds (butchers) with whom George stayed on his arrival from Rugby where he had been a mechanic for United Dairies. This hut utilised the yard of the Bell Inn, a space that had come to be occupied by caravans at the time of the October Banbury Fairs.

He lived on the other side of the road in a lovely little house close to Strouds the butchers. It was owned by the Orchards.

Apart from cars, Mumford's big business was the changing of radio accumulators. Each morning there would be a procession of people along the Middleton Raod. Amazingly they were able to identify their own accumulators.

On Sunday afternoons, George along with his friends and business acquaintances would often have trips out by car to places of interest.

One of the many outing parties: Back row: George Mumford, Miss Jarvis (Middleton Cheney), Amy Mumford (George's wife), Bill Battley (a postman), Mr. Hale and son Eric [Hale had the Parsons Street bicycle shop], Mrs. Hale, Bill Stroud. Centre row: Mrs. Jelfs (wife of Parson's Street butcher), Emily Stroud, Ron Battley, Evelyn Stroud (daughter of Bill). Front row: Mr. Jelfs [butcher], Harry Stroud, Gerald Jarvis (butcher at Middleton Cheney)

When Mumford finished with the business, Tommy Gascoigne took over. George retired to a house opposite the Lido pool with a large garden and hard tennis courts.

Equally a personality but in a very different line of business was William McKeever, a scrap metal merchant. He and his wife had a very fine house and yard. Many people remember him because he would buy rabbit skins, though not always for as much as you anticipated. Mary McKeever had a hairdressing business over the workshop.

Exciting moment for Mumford's garage — arrival of steam engine owned by J. Russell, local photographer.

Bakeries

Up to the outbreak of the Second World War, bakers performed an important social function in addition to the production of bread. Because few people had gas ovens, traders such as Frank Eeles of the Causeway cooked Sunday dinner in their bread ovens.

Frank and his wife outside their shop which sold groceries and was licensed for tobacco. Sharp-eyed readers will spot tins of Coleman's mustard and packets of Lux soap flakes amongst the various items on window display. Date of picture about 1913.

Certain bakers like Eeles took customers' dough and, within two hours, transformed it into cakes. Others such as Jack Taylor of Old Grimsbury Road had a line popular with children. Jack's 1d. cottage loaves were eagerly snapped up.

Lay and Molyneux (Old Grimsbury Road), Thornton (North Street) and Somerton and Jelfs (South Street) are other well-remembered small bakers.

Prior to Ray Malcolm at Middleton Road, Powell and then Warren managed successful enterprises. The former was a big man who usually sported a trilby. Apart from the shop he delivered in Grimsbury and in the rural areas around and was fired with the belief that shop owners belonged to a higher social order than most people in the locality. Apart from baking bread he was a Grimsbury property owner who always collected rents on a Monday.

Powell was succeeded by Fergie Warren, seen in the shop photograph and alongside Ray Malcolm.

Looking across the counter are from left to right: Helen Mayall (office clerk), Zena Edge (made the sandwiches), Shirley Ford, Janet Hale, Fergie Warren, Ada Phipps, Joyce Brown, and Ray Malcolm.

Fergie had built up previous baking experience at Shotteswell near Banbury. Grimsbury was a logical choice for trading as his parents lived in West Street. In addition there was Ada Phipps to drive a small van for him.

In January 1975 Raymond Malcolm took over the bakery and the shop but soon gave up deliveries in Grimsbury. He had come in to the trade because of family experience in Birmingham. Ada Phipps gave him good support until her retirement.

Ada's retirement is celebrated left to right: Paul Baker, Chris Phipps (her husband), Ada, Zena Edge (her husband's mother was a licencee of the Cricketers), Shirley Ford (Ada's niece), Ray Malcolm and Helen Mayall.

68   CHANGING FACES OF GRIMSBURY

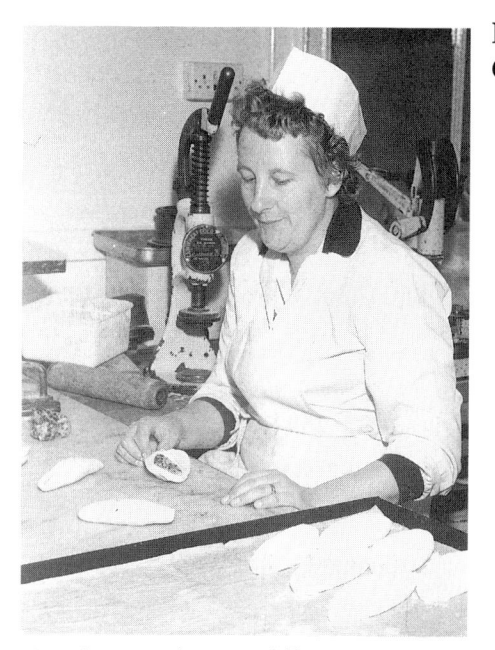

Ray continued the local reputation for Banbury Cakes. (*Courtesy of the late Michael Gee*)

Carol Hawkin's fills Banbury Cakes.

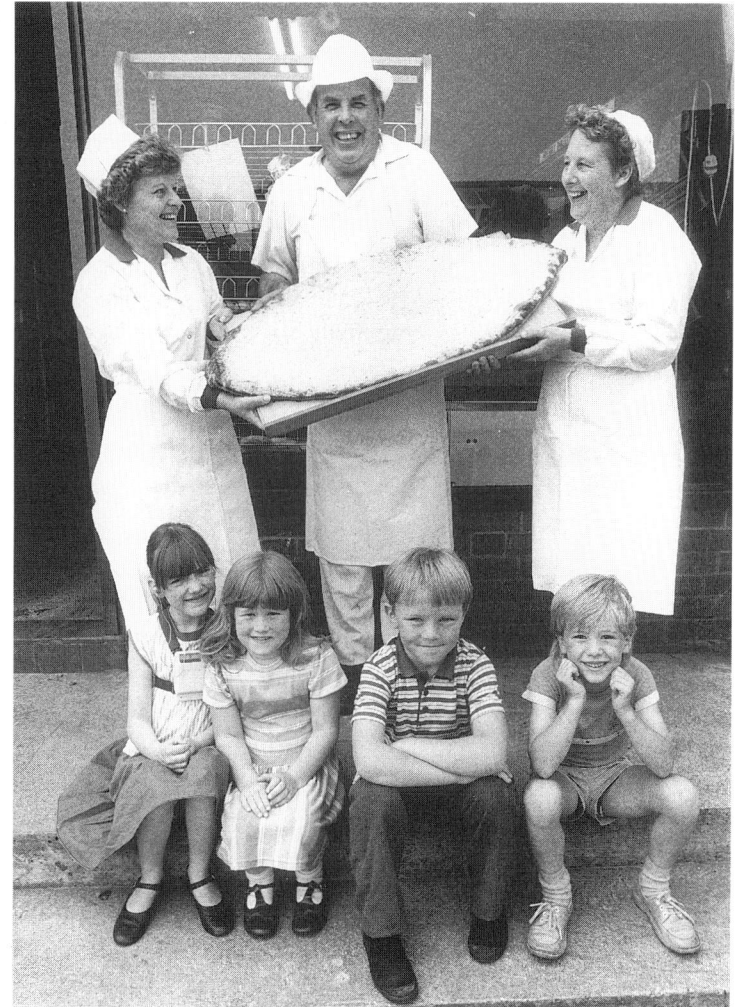

Happiness is a large Banbury Cake. Ray Malcolm flanked by Pamela Jarvis (now Cox) on his left and Carol Hawkins on the right.

PLACES OF WORK 69

Jean Young (stayed some ten years) behind the till and flanked by an impressive display of cakes and pastries.

Hugh Scully with a plate of Ray's Banbury Cakes at a Spiceball Park "Antiques Roadshow" of 1985. "Not antique, freshly baked of course!"

70 CHANGING FACES OF GRIMSBURY

Close up of shop exterior.

At the end of 1998, Ray Malcolm closed his Middleton Road bakery and associated shops. This was the last in a long line of such businesses which had been family run and mostly operated out of rooms in terraced houses in Grimsbury.

Ray's distinct bag design.

R.S. Malcolm
Family Baker
Banbury Cakes

41 HIGH STREET AND
53 MIDDLETON ROAD
BANBURY

0295
257724

One of the last trays of Banbury Cakes before closure.

Sonia Pratt, sales assistant, gazes wistfully at the shop display of cakes.

SECTION SIX

Religion and Education

In nineteenth century, Grimsbury, Methodism and Elementary Education went hand in hand. A chapel with Sunday School incorporated was built in North Street in 1858. It appears to have been a response to the emergence of New Grimsbury between that street and the Middleton Road.

Early signs were encouraging with 102 children recorded. The staff consisted of E. J. Payne (the Superintendent) and eight teachers, five of whom were male. Summer treats were organised jointly with Banbury Methodists and, on special occasions, these groups came together at the Church Lane Chapel.

Views of what remains of the chapel (beyond the archway).

RELIGION AND EDUCATION 73

By 1871 the size of the Methodist Society locally necessitated new premises which were opened in West Street. Half the cost of this combined Chapel and Sunday School was met by that prominent local methodist philanthropist William Mewburn of Wykham Park.

Five years later, a larger schoolroom had been constructed so that the original space for children could be made part of a church for 300 people.

Above: The foundation stone commemorating the link with Mewburn.

Exterior view of the Wesleyan Church in West Street, Grimsbury.

Interior view of this church.

During the two World Wars of the present century, the church premises were devoted to other purposes. Between 1915 and 1919 the Red Cross Hospital was located here with injured service personnel being transported from the railway station.

Staff and patients at the Red Cross Hospital.

Different uses of the building coincided with the more recent war. It was a reception centre for people affected by bomb raids, and rooms were taken over by Banbury Grammar School (due to a fire) and by St. Leonard's School because of lack of primary level accommodation until 1954

The minute book for the Grimsbury Methodists which covers the post war years from 1960 to 1993 provides some excellent insights into the life of the West Street Church.

RELIGION AND EDUCATION   75

The 1960s seem to have been a decade of change and difficulties. In 1962, there was still a core of trustees, mainly business people. These included Mark Trinder (Banbury Council foreman), Reginald Adams (maltster), Sidney Cherry (Cropredy builder), William Paxman (Director of the Banbury Butter Company), and Luke Coleman (shop manager with the Banbury and District Co-operative Society). In the ranks of the new trustees at that time were Leonard How (a clerk), William Slatter (a school caretaker), John Lickorish (coal loader), Lesley Tanner (a postman) and Grace Jelfs (housewife).

Grace Jelfs with husband Don outside the East Street School at the outset of his mayoral year. Both were pillars of West Street Church.

The key problems facing this very able committee were especially to do with the deteriorating fabric of the church and the inadequacy of the heating (mal-functioning of tortoise stoves!). There were also issues about recruitment of a new organist and the need to maintain the Methodist right of access to Moorfields. Persistence of a gate at the rear of the chapel cost one shilling a year.

A valuable source of income came from lettings of the school room. The local uniformed brigades, Grimsbury Badminton Club, a Boxing Club and a Pigeon Club were typical users though not without a few hiccups.

In the 1970s discussions focussed on a new building and the Borough Council was approached about dual purpose status. Talks took place with St. Leonard's Church committee concerning shared facilities especially during any construction period. This was also the time of the centenary celebrations.

WELCOME BY THE CHAIRMAN The Minister ... ... Rev. Mark Alsop **GREETINGS** *From the Borough:* The Deputy Mayor ... ... Councillor F. Partridge *From the Oxford and Leicester District:* Chairman of the District Rev. Gordon W. Argyle, B.D. *From Other Denominations:* The Vicar of Banbury ... ... Rev. Ian Beecham *From the Banbury Circuit:* Senior Circuit Steward ... ... Mr. Len How *Reply on behalf of the Church:* County Councillor ... ... Mrs. Grace Jelfs	*MENU* SOUP —:— TURKEY and HAM SALAD —:— TRIFLE —:— CHEESE and BISCUITS —:— COFFEE

Dinner menu.

When Miss A.T.V. opened the Bazaar of 7th November 1981, it was possible to display a plan of the re-development and to think about auctioning parts of the old building to raise money.

In 1986 the new church together with adjacent Methodist housing opened. It was the culmination of some 115 years of existence in West street and a watershed in the history of Grimsbury Methodism. Above all it was a tribute to tireless workers like Jack Lickorish (oldest surviving member of the coal merchant and shop businesses, Nellie How (champion fund raiser based on her cooking prowess), Len How (Nellie's brother), Eileen Ward-Smith, Ernie Barnes and Clara Slatter.

RELIGION AND EDUCATION   77

The old church being demolished.

The new church.

West Court – Methodist Homes for the elderly.

A hundred pupils were registered at a Wesleyan day school which opened in February 1881 and occupied West Street premises.

By Easter of that year, the first head was in post — he was James Dommett. Under his leadership, expansion was immediate and, by June, 211 pupils were on the roll.

Continued expansion of the Grimsbury area meant a growth in demand for school places. Not surprisingly by 1890 extensive renovation of the premises was necessary and a lecture room was converted to an infant school.

In 1909, the Banbury Advertiser for 28th October covered the story of how the Wesleyans had a new building erected by Higgs of Northampton in the road that became School View.

Cost of this development was just over £6,000 but the relocation was considered controversial because of the size of the construction bill.

Alderman James Picton and Henry Staveley Hill performed the stone laying ceremony which was followed by a champagne lunch in a marquee. This event marked not only the transition of educational provision from West Street to School View but also the transfer of organisational responsibility from the Wesleyans to the Borough Council which had become the Local Education Authority for elementary education under the Education Act of 1902.

An early group photograph taken at the rear of the Council School. Third from the left in the back row is Mary Offord.

Modern housing on the School View site.

RELIGION AND EDUCATION   79

At the time of the 1998 demolition work on the School View site, the foundation stones were saved and erected as a monument in the grounds of the new school just off the Overthorpe Road.

Foundation stones from the School View building form a monument at the new location.

The new school off the Overthorpe Road.

The catchment for the 1909 school was especially Merton Street and the Causeway area. Many of the people in these streets were chapel folk and so the link with Methodism was retained. At the outset there was education for children between the ages of 3 and 14. Enid Beere recalls how her brother, when 3½ years old, was admitted to the babies' class in 1925. Special equipment was made available to this group which included rocking horses and a sand tray.

With family hardship very much a characteristic of Grimsbury in the 1920s and 1930s, there were few opportunities for education beyond age 14 and certainly none in the area. The importance of a decision of the Blue Coat Foundation Trustees in May 1930 cannot be under-estimated. At a meeting held in St. Mary's Church House, Tom Homer (Post Office clerk and Council representative) proposed that the Trustees should finance two exhibitions for local school pupils. Each was to be worth "An annual sum of £11 or such additional sums as the Trustees may decide".

Robert Luscombe, early 1930s headmaster of Banbury County (later Grammar) School.

The outcome of an examination set and marked by Robert Luscombe headmaster of Banbury County (later Grammar) School was that both awards went to pupil's of Grimsbury School. Ismay Ellen Jarvis and Sylvia Dean were from Centre Street and the Middleton Road respectively. Out of 211 marks, Ismay scored 160 and Sylvia 194.

Subsequent minutes make it possible to follow the progress of the girls to the County School whose administrators were allowed further money for their uniforms. The question then arose of the Centre Street pupil getting to Easington and it is interesting to note that the Trustees permitted a portion of the money to be spent on a bicycle.

It appears that both girls did very well at their new school. This prompted the Blue Coat Guardians to extend the awards until Ismay and Sylvia reached the age of 18 with the built in clause that neither changed status to that of pupil teacher.

In 1944 Grimsbury Council School became an 11 to 14 establishment. Out of all the head teachers, perhaps the one who has lived the longest in local memories is Norman Scroxton. He was able to identify with the pupils through his informal approach which was typified by his participation in playground activities. In summer, Norman's set of stumps was the basis of informal cricket but at all seasons he was proud of the official school sports teams.

RELIGION AND EDUCATION

Names that stood out of the staff list at St Leonards were Miss Watts and Mr. Spicer. The latter organised the very popular May Festival.

Miss Watts 2A class on a day in the 1950s at St Leonards when flu ravaged the school. Left to right: David Meadows, David Viner, Shirley Barnes, Wendy Clargo.

Photograph of Enid Beere's colleagues at Grimsbury Secondary Modern School in mid-sixties: Back row left to right: Sam Raby, Brian Greaves, Keith Howell, Norman Hamer Middle row: Mrs. Golding, Mrs. Tooth (secretary), Mrs. Adcock, Mrs. Sheila Haynes. Front row: Sid (Killer) Jones [woodwork], Miss Wilkes (Senior Mistress), Jack Burden, Mrs. Perchard, Mrs. Reeve.

Twenty years later, in 1967 when Comprehensive secondary education was introduced to the town, it turned into Grimsbury Hall as Banbury School under Harry Judge developed into a federation of halls.

The significance of links between education and religion can also be identified within the Anglican Church. On 11th July 1891, St. Leonard's Church was consecrated as a chapel-of-ease and daughter institution of Christ Church, South Banbury.

St. Leonard's choir in 1918.

The building was constructed on glebe land in the Middleton Road where centuries earlier there stood a leper hospital known as St. Leonard's.

The act of consecration was performed by Dr. Stubbs, Bishop of Oxford, in front of a very modest congregation. Possibly Saturday was inconvenient for many people.

In 1921 separate parish status was granted and with it John Frederick Nutthall as the first vicar (1921-26). Two years later the adjacent school, which had been established by Christ Church as a National School in 1862, became St. Leonard's Grimsbury Church of England School.

A Beale's photograph of Christ Church (later St. Leonard's School.

RELIGION AND EDUCATION

Standard IV Class Christ Church School 1908.

The building today, part used as a health and fitness centre.

An aerial view of the Infant School before 1960. Note the spacious grounds and the allotments in the foreground. Much of the space has been built on (East Close bungalows) and the allotments have gone.

84   CHANGING FACES OF GRIMSBURY

Grimsbury Infants moved into a new East Street school in 1957. Brenda Lukasinska became its head three years later. By the time she retired in 1978 the school had become multi-cultural.

Mrs. Lukasinska's Class of 1978: front left to front right Andrew Lee, Rajinder Dhuggo, Wendy Broughton, Alastair Allen. Jeffrey Smith, Stuart Herring, Mark Herbert, Khalid Mahmood, Lauren Horne, Brenda Lukasinska, Bharbinder Atwah, Kathleen Hughes, Martin Trusler, Stephen Hopkins, Martin Hedges. The other member of the class, Jeffrey Young, was absent. Predominantly the Asian children were from Pakistan and were of the Muslim faith.

The school consisted of four classes, sometimes of up to 40 children, but only gained a nursery group after 1978. In Brenda's time the day began with an assembly of the whole school, the organisation of which owed as much to the pupils as to the staff.

Parents have always come along to the school for such occasions as Nativity Plays and summer shows but it was only from the late seventies that some were active within the establishment by helping with cookery.

By the time Isabelle Brown became head of school in 1982, the multi-cultural nature of its roll was especially evident in the addition of Eid celebrations to mark the conclusion of Ramadan. Games were played and the food consumed included a number of Pakistani dishes.

RELIGION AND EDUCATION 85

Summer Concert.

A Nativity Play at East Street Infants.

Another festive occasion was in May when East Street infants revived the English custom of dancing around maypoles. Gradually this occasion became less dominated by the crowning of May Kings and Queens and more characterised by a programme of music and dancing. The school put this on towards half-term whereas St. Leonard's had a festival on 1st May.

St. Leonard's School May festival 1950/51.

An earlier cause for celebration, St. Leonard's School, V.E. Day 1945.

A good link with the older members of the Grimsbury community was forged at harvest time when the older children accompanied by parents conveyed produce to elderly people.

An important role for the school in the eighties and early nineties was enhancement of life experiences for many children, who unlike earlier generations were unaware of the immediate countryside beyond Grimsbury and had not enjoyed visits to places like Guiting Powers (Rare Breeds Centre), Warwick Park and Whipsnade Zoo. The school outing was firmly in the curriculum.

Significant developments also took place at the church. In 1926 there was the construction of the Lady Chapel.

A member of the choir between 1927 and 1933 was Ron Battley. He remembers those days for many reasons. Firstly he was about to emerge from the probationer phase when a Saturday night fire caused postponement of his first service as a fully fledged choir boy. Indeed for some six months services were held in the church hall made of corrugated iron.

Choir outings were an annual treat and never more so than when the choir members were allowed to vote on the venue. Boys outnumbered men and they all finished up at Swindon Railway Works where the boys indulged themselves in engine spotting.

Sunday services sometimes contained a particularly tedious and lengthy sermon by the then incumbent Revd. Diamond. However if the boys started mumbling, Diamond would swing round in the pulpit and exhort them to keep quiet.

A staunch supporter of the choir was the organist, Lydia Anne Dwyer, wife of Dr. Hubert Dwyer who practised in the Middleton Road. Every Christmas she gave a present to each of the choir boys.

An early thirties wedding at St. Leonard's when Henry Higham married a Miss Wilkins from the Causeway. Left to right: Sister of the bride, Ellen Higham, Robert Higham, Alice Kitely Higham, the bridegroom ,the bride, Harold Higham, ?, parents of the bride.

In St. Leonard's magazine for July 1931 it is recorded that the Rev. John Nutthall had Passion Pictures in the nave. Each of the originals was a gift from an individual or group of people associated with the church. The intention was to have memorials of relatives and friends killed in the Great War or to establish tokens of gratitude for their safe return.

Sadly a fire had destroyed many of the originals (the same fire referred to by Ron Battley). However Hildred Herpin of the Royal College of Art in London was commissioned to produce fourteen pictures capable of being attached to the Stations of the Cross.

Much later in the 1950s the Reredos was erected as a memorial to Colonel Edmunds of Hunt Edmunds Brewery who had been a regular worshipper.

The electoral roll for the church in 1970 shows that the congregation was drawn from all over Grimsbury. However the area from the Middleton Road to Grimsbury Green and Manor Road was better represented than the roads to the east of it.

1977 was the year Grimsbury Parish was united with the Benefice of St. Mary. This was the start of the team ministry in Banbury and a year later Robert George Rhodes (now at Milton Keynes) became the first Team Vicar of St. Leonard's. Tony Greenfield and then Andrew Milton took on the mantle in 1982 and 1987 respectively.

Left to right: Peter Beck, David Meikle, Peter Haynes and Bob Rhodes, members of the Banbury Team Ministry make the most of a Christmas pantomime performance in Church House, Horse Fair, Banbury.

Since the 1970s, Grimsbury has both expanded rapidly and become more multi-cultural in character with thriving Muslim and Sikh communities. In a time of change, St. Leonard's Church has managed to remain a focal point in its area. Annual events such as the summer fetes and special occasions like the opening of St. Leonard's New Hall in 1975, the 21st Birthday of the local Women's Fellowship and particularly the centenary celebrations in 1991 were attended by young and old, lifelong members of St. Leonard's and alongside them members of ethnic groups. Some fetes under the banner of "Blow Your Own Trumpet" were organised in such a way as to attract groups from a wide cross section of the Grimsbury community and from further afield.

RELIGION AND EDUCATION 89

1975 — New Hall opened by Neil Marten M.P. Mayor, Don Jelfs, who was also a local councillor welcomes him.

1976 — Congregation enters church for Palm Sunday Service.

1979 – Gipsy Fete left to right: Rosemary Popplewell, Gill Proudfoot, Rev'd Bob Rhodes.

Blow Your Own Trumpet – July 1983 – vicarage garden.

RELIGION AND EDUCATION 91

Balwinder Singh with Mike Snelling, Community Policeman, at same event.

Children at same event.

Members of St. Leonard's Women's Fellowship at 21st Birthday Party — 1985.

Women's Fellowship 21st Birthday Party: Mrs. Bettie Hood (3rd from left), Rev'd Raymond Haynes, Rev'd Tony Boult (former vicars).

St. Leonard's Church has outlived both Christ Church which was demolished in 1967 and St. Leonard's School. The former school building in the Middleton Road is home to a health and fitness centre and has a base for the St. John's Ambulance Brigade.

Today Father Bruce Walls finds himself in a Church that is once again the centre of a parish in its own right.

July 1991 — St. Leonard's Centenary Celebrations: Rev'd Andrew Milton, Team Vicar, with Right Rev'd Anthony Russell, Bishop of Dorchester.

St. Leonard's congregation in 1991.

St. Leonard's Church Notice board late 1998.

Members of the Sikh community, well remembered for their links with St. Leonard's Church, are mainly living away from Grimsbury but come together for worship at their temple in West Street (adjoining the Methodist Church). By contrast there are considerable numbers of Pakistani Muslims with property in most streets within the traditional part of Grimsbury. Few work in the area though there is a small store in East Street that is Muslim owned and stocks Asian groceries.

Most early arrivals in the area were men on their own and they came in the early sixties. Their first Mosque was in North Street.

By the 1970s and 1980s families were in evidence and it became increasingly important to establish a permanent Mosque with a range of facilities. For a time a house in Castle Street met their needs but in 1990/1991 permission was secured to develop in Merton Street. Here the building holds up to 300 people and there is also provision for the education of children from the age of five.

The outside of the Merton Street Mosque. In the car park left to right: Safraz Bhatti, Abdul Khaliq, Mazar Choudhary, Saeed Choudhary.

Worship in progress at Merton Street Mosque.

Worshippers around the Iman (seated).

Postscript

Separated from Banbury by the River Cherwell, Oxford Canal and the railway, Grimsbury can justifiably claim existence as a separate entity. Indeed there are those who would go so far as to suggest "home rule".

Recent loss of the Banbury Stockyard from its Merton Street location combined with the emergence of new housing and industry especially towards the M40 motorway has had a profound effect on life and perceptions. Traditional ways of living have become old ways. With the closure of Malcolms bakery in the Middleton Road a whole era of reliance on local bakehouses has gone. The successful Co-op in the Middleton Road is an even more distant memory. For the Grimsbury person of 1999 "Sharing and Caring" has been replaced by "Eight till late" with the arrival of businesses like Alldays.

The name of "Stroud" is still well-known but Grimsbury is no longer the domain of the railway worker, Northern Aluminium personnel or indeed those who served the Britannia Works, Henry Stone and Switchgear.

People of Asian origin have added a new dimension to almost all aspects of life in the area, not least the small shop ownership.

The Bowling Green, Blacklocks, Bell, Cricketers and Elephant and Castle have been joined by the Pepper Pot but last orders have been called at the Prince of Wales in Centre Street. There all is silent except for the workman's hammer and a voice in our ear that still wants to say, "Good Night Wally".